MW00469323

The Joan Palevsky Imprint in Classical Literature

In honor of beloved Virgil—

"O degli altri poeti onore e lume . . ."

—Dante, *Inferno*

The publisher gratefully acknowledges the generous support of the Classical Literature Endowment Fund of the University of California Press Foundation, which was established by a major gift from Joan Palevsky.

The Complete Poems of Tibullus

The Complete Poems of Tibullus

An En Face Bilingual Edition

ALBIUS TIBULLUS,
LYGDAMUS, AND
SULPICIA

Translated by Rodney G. Dennis and Michael C. J. Putnam
With an Introduction by Julia Haig Gaisser

University of California Press   Berkeley Los Angeles London

University of California Press, one of the most distinguished univer-
sity presses in the United States, enriches lives around the world by
advancing scholarship in the humanities, social sciences, and natural
sciences. Its activities are supported by the UC Press Foundation and
by philanthropic contributions from individuals and institutions.
For more information, visit www.ucpress.edu.

University of California Press
Berkeley and Los Angeles, California
University of California Press, Ltd.
London, England

© 2012 by The Regents of the University of California

Library of Congress Cataloging-in-Publication Data

Tibullus.
  [Poems. English & Latin].
  The complete poems of Tibullus : an en face bilingual edition /
Albius Tibullus, Lygdamus, and Sulpicia ; translated by Rodney G.
Dennis and Michael C.J. Putnam ; with an introduction by Julia
Haig Gaisser
      p. cm.
  Includes bibliographical references and index.
  ISBN 978-0-520-27253-8 (cloth, alk. paper) —
ISBN 978-0-520-27254-5 (pbk., alk. paper)
  1. Tibullus—Translations into English.   I. Dennis, Rodney G.
II. Putnam, Michael C.J.   III. Title.
PA6788.E5D46 2012
874'.01—dc23   2011044244

Manufactured in the United States of America

21 20 19 18 17 16 15 14 13 12 11
10 9 8 7 6 5 4 3 2 1

In keeping with its commitment to support environmentally
responsible and sustainable printing practices, UC Press has printed
this book on Cascades Enviro 100, a 100% post–consumer waste,
recycled, de-inked fiber. FSC recycled, certified, and processed
chlorine-free. It is acid-free, Ecologo-certified, and manufactured
by BioGas Energy.

For Joseph Farrell

Contents

Preface

Rodney Dennis died on October 12, 2006. He had been working at his translation of Tibullus for some time and had submitted it for consideration to the University of California Press early in the previous year. In the months before his unexpected death he asked me in conversation if I would be willing to provide an introduction, and he expressed the hope to work with Julia Haig Gaisser at perfecting the manuscript. These roles have now been reversed. Professor Gaisser presents Tibullus and his poetry to us in the introduction. I have assumed the pleasant burden, with her encouragement and unstinting help, of revising the manuscript, in many instances substantially, while also adding the poetry of Lygdamus and Sulpicia. I have taken the readers' reports into account but attempted the while to preserve the unaffected, immediate tone that Rodney Dennis set in his initial rendering of this great poet, which makes him so congenial to readers.

Together he and I have tried to convey the sense in English of the only meter that Tibullus uses, the elegiac couplet. This consists of an hexameter, which is to say a six-foot line utilizing dactyls and spondees, followed by a pentameter, a line with a total of five feet that twice repeats the initial two and a half feet of the preceding hexameter. The meters of Latin poetry, however, are quantitative, whereas English poetry depends largely on accent and rhyme. Our attempt to find a modern equivalent of Tibullus's often brilliant metrical effects is to utilize couplets that consist of a flexible, essentially six-beat line followed by a more unvarying verse, normally with five accents. Rhyme does not become a regular part of Latin verse construction until the hymns of St. Ambrose, written in the second half of the fourth century C.E. With only occasional exceptions I have shied away from its deliberate use save in final couplets, where it serves as a bow to the English sense of an ending.*

---

*See Barbara Herrnstein Smith, *Poetic Closure: A Study of How Poems End* (Chicago, 1968), 47–48, 51–53, 70–79.

Two further points. I have avoided archaisms wherever possible in an attempt to reproduce, in contemporary English, Tibullus's immediate, unpretentious, but deceptively simple style. I have also endeavored to suggest aspects of that style that help differentiate him from his fellow Roman elegists Propertius and Ovid. One of these is his penchant for verbal repetition, which, always gracefully employed, serves as perhaps his poetry's greatest single unifying force. I have also kept ancient place names wherever possible, even when the modern equivalent would be clear.

Thanks are due to many friends and scholars for deepening my understanding of Tibullus over the years. Lee Pearcy helped me to read Sulpicia better. Eric Schmidt of the University of California Press was most supportive at every stage of production. Paul Psoinos served as a model copyeditor—as judicious and discerning as he was scrupulous. I owe a special debt of gratitude to the two readers for the press, Eleanor Winsor Leach and one who remains anonymous. Both saved me from many infelicities while in the process appending equally numerous suggestions that have richly enhanced the enterprise. I am most grateful. The remaining faults are mine.

Michael C. J. Putnam
Rockport, Maine
August 2011

Introduction

Tibullus has left us just sixteen elegies. Their subjects are various: love (of the fickle girls Delia and Nemesis and of the equally fickle boy Marathus), hatred of war, praise of his friend and patron, Messalla Corvinus,[1] the pleasures of rural simplicity, a celebration of Rome. His poems glide easily, some would say dreamily, from theme to theme, moving almost like a slide show through apparently random images and musings. The ancient critic Quintilian considered Tibullus "the most polished and elegant" of the Roman elegists.[2] He is also the most artful. His randomness and dreaminess are carefully created illusions; the elegance and polish so admired by Quintilian are achieved with intention and consummate skill. Tibullus's artistry is more subtle than that of the other elegists—we could almost call it clandestine. Propertius, notoriously difficult, displays his learning and emotional complexity with allusions to Callimachus, jumps in thought, and elaborate mythological exempla. Ovid is smooth and ostentatiously clever—a witty master of language who is self-consciously playful both in and out of season. Tibullus, by contrast, never advertises. He is as learned and witty as either of his fellow elegists, and with emotional depths of his own, but his is the art that conceals, rather than reveals, its powers. He is a poet in whom everything seems accessible, on the surface—and in whom there is always more to discover.

We know almost nothing about Tibullus's life. His family name was probably Albius.[3] His first name is unknown. He perhaps had a villa near the old

---

1. Marcus Valerius Messalla Corvinus, 64 B.C.E.–8 C.E.

2. Quintilian's comment comes from his famous pronouncement on the elegists: "In elegy too we challenge the Greeks. Tibullus seems to me its most polished and elegant author. Some prefer Propertius. Ovid is more frivolous than either, just as Gallus is more severe" (*Institutio oratoria* 10.1.93).

3. Horace addresses two poems to an elegist he calls Albius (*Ode* 1.33, *Epistle* 1.4). Critics in antiquity identified Albius as Tibullus, and the name Albius Tibullus also appears in most of the manuscripts.

town of Pedum, not far from Rome.[4] He was probably born between 55 and 48 B.C.E., and according to the verses of the Augustan epigrammatist Domitius Marsus, he died not long after Virgil, sometime after September of 19:

> You were still a young man, Tibullus, but unjust Mors
>   Sent you to the Elysian Fields as Virgil's companion,
> That none should be left to weep soft loves in elegies
>   Or to sing battles of kings in powerful measures.

Ovid provides a longer epitaph; his lament in *Amores* 3.9, both witty and moving, is translated below in the appendix. Tibullus claims to be poor ("Let my poverty direct me through a lazy life," he says in *Elegy* 1.1.5); but he was by no means indigent. Horace calls him handsome and rich: "The gods have given you good looks; the gods have given you wealth and the art of enjoyment," he reminds Tibullus in *Epistle* 1.4.6–7. An ancient life of the poet identifies him as a Roman *eques* or knight, a rank of very high social standing and requiring a minimum property qualification of 400,000 sesterces.[5] Perhaps Tibullus's property was less than that of his ancestors, as he asserts in *Elegy* 1.1, and it may well have suffered in the land confiscations of the 40s and 30s, although he does not say so; but then as now it was a convention for poets to be poor: in the previous generation, for example, the wealthy Catullus claimed a "purse full of cobwebs" (*Carm.* 13.8). Like most young men of his class, Tibullus would have been expected to undertake a public career, the first step of which would have been serving on the staff of a general or provincial governor. In Tibullus's case the general turned out to be Valerius Messalla Corvinus, under whom he served on at least one campaign, as he tells us in *Elegies* 1.3 and 1.7.[6] He found the military life uncongenial (see especially *Elegies* 1.1 and 1.10), but in his poetry he celebrates Messalla as both a great man and a friend.

THE WORLD OF THE ROMAN ELEGISTS

Tibullus lived in what the old Chinese curse would call "interesting times." He was just a child when Julius Caesar was assassinated in 44, but he would

---

4. In *Epistle* 1.4.2 Horace speaks of Albius as spending time "in the district of Pedum" ("in regione Pedana").

5. The life appears with Domitius Marsus's epigram in the earliest manuscripts, and it is generally thought to be derived from Suetonius's lost work *On the Poets* (*De poetis*). Both the epigram and the life are printed in most Latin editions of Tibullus. For the property qualification, see Taylor.

6. For Messalla, see Syme, *Augustan Aristocracy* 200–226; Butrica.

have been old enough to be well aware of (and no doubt affected by) the terrible violence and upheavals that ravaged Italy for many years while the warring triumvirate of Octavian, Lepidus, and Antony battled first the assassins and then each other as they struggled for supremacy. He grew up surrounded by civil war, proscriptions, confiscations of land, and countless acts of random and intentional violence. As a young man he would have seen the end of the struggle and the beginning of the new order that would be called the Augustan age. Octavian finally defeated Antony in the battle of Actium in 31; he inaugurated his regime with the celebration of a triple triumph in 29 and took the title Augustus in 27.

Whatever else it was, the Augustan era was an age of brilliant poets. Virgil, Horace, Tibullus, Propertius, and Ovid all produced masterpieces in the first decade or so of the new regime. The short period from 31 to 19 saw Virgil's *Georgics* and *Aeneid,* Horace's *Epodes,* three books of his *Odes,* and the first book of his *Epistles,* Tibullus's elegies, three books of Propertius's elegies, and the first edition of Ovid's *Amores.*[7] All these poets were influenced by the struggles of the 40s and 30s and the final concentration of absolute power in Augustus.

Virgil (b. 70) and Horace (b. 65) lived through the whole period as adults, and both the trauma and their complex responses to it are reflected in their poetry of the 40s and 30s. Virgil grieves for the land confiscations in his poignant *Eclogues* 1 and 9 but also treats Octavian as a god in *Eclogue* 1 and *Georgics* 1 and 3. Horace despairs of a society torn by civil war in *Epodes* 7 and 16 but celebrates the battle of Actium in *Epodes* 1 and 9. At some point in the 30s both poets came to the notice of Maecenas, who was Octavian's partisan and agent but also a highly cultivated student of poetry. They enjoyed Maecenas's friendship and support for the rest of their lives (he gave Horace his famous Sabine farm), but the extent of his direct influence on their work is unclear. Maecenas undoubtedly talked to them about Octavian's (later Augustus's) political and cultural aspirations, but he did not dictate the way they approached the themes of their poetry.[8] The poems of Virgil and Horace in the 20s praise the new imperial Rome and its *princeps* Augustus, and do so in nuanced ways that evoke different and often completely opposing interpretations from modern readers. The *Aeneid* and the *Odes* are sometimes seen as triumphalist (some would say sycophantic)

7. The *Georgics* were largely written in the 30s B.C.E. but were completed after Actium. Horace's *Epodes* include poems written both before and after Actium.
8. For an excellent discussion of the roles of poets and patrons, see White, esp. 3–34.

glorifications of Augustus's achievements, sometimes—and this is particularly the case with the *Aeneid*—as dark appraisals of them. In fact, these works of Horace and Virgil are indissoluble compounds of praise, sadness, hope, and loss—just as we might expect from poets of their genius and sensibility who had lived through dark days of violence and disorder to see the imposition of a stable, productive, and absolutist peace.

Tibullus and Propertius came of age only with the beginning of the new era. Ovid, born in 43 (the only one of the Augustan poets to be born after Caesar's assassination), was not yet a teenager at the time of Actium. All three began their literary careers in the 20s, and all in the genre of elegy. To put it another way, we could say that elegy was the genre of the poets who started their careers under the new regime.

Elegy is a very broad category: regardless of subject, any poem in elegiac couplets longer than eighteen or twenty lines or so is ipso facto an elegy.[9] The genre was used by Greek poets of both the archaic and Hellenistic periods, as well as by Catullus in the 50s B.C.E.[10] The particular form found in the Augustan elegists is different from both its Greek and its Catullan antecedents but has elements of both in its DNA. We would be in a better position to understand its origins and development if we had the work of its earliest practitioner, the fourth Augustan elegist, Gaius Cornelius Gallus (d. 27/6). Gallus (b. 70/69), a contemporary of Virgil, began writing in the 30s and perhaps as early as the late 40s, producing four books of elegies to a woman he called Lycoris (an actress named Volumnia Cytheris, who had also been the mistress of Antony). Gallus was an important and influential poet (Virgil honors him in *Eclogues* 6 and 10, for example); but unfortunately only ten verses of his poetry survive—too little to give more than a few hints of his contributions to the genre.[11]

The best way to understand why the Augustan elegists chose their genre is to see what they did with it.[12] Although each elegist is different, the genre has certain defining characteristics.

Its principal theme is love of an unattainable or only rarely attained

---

9. For a description of the elegiac meter, see the preface. Shorter poems in couplets are called epigrams, but it is not always easy to distinguish between a short elegy and a long epigram.

10. Catullus has four elegies (*Carmina* 65–68), very different from each other in subject and tone.

11. For Gallus and his poetry, see Hollis 219–52.

12. For excellent discussions, all with earlier bibliography, see Cairns, *Tibullus* 214–30; James 3–34; Miller, *Subjecting Verses* 1–30.

woman, always called a "girl" (*puella*), who has other lovers. The subject is a genetic inheritance from the Lesbia poetry of Catullus, but it is radically transformed in elegy. Catullus depicts an adulterous affair with an aristocratic Roman matron, Clodia, for whom he uses the metrically equivalent pseudonym Lesbia. Lesbia is named for Sappho, the great poet of Lesbos, and Catullus suggests that she shares the elegance and literary taste of her namesake. He presents himself as an emotionally engaged but painfully disillusioned lover, broken by her careless promiscuity but unable to break away. As he says in *Carmen* 85:

> I hate, and I love. Perhaps you ask why I do this.
> I do not know, but I feel it happening, and I am in torment.

Elegy takes place in a different world. Its girls are not slumming aristocrats like Lesbia but courtesans, stock characters derived by way of Gallus's Lycoris from the courtesans of comedy and mime.[13] Like Lesbia, most have names with a literary flavor. The name Lycoris is derived from Lycoreus, a cult title of Apollo, the god of poetry.[14] Propertius's Cynthia takes her name from a place associated with Apollo, as does Tibullus's Delia. (Apollo was born near Mount Cynthus, on the island of Delos.) Although Tibullus deviates from the pattern with the ominous name of Delia's successor, Nemesis, Ovid's girl is named for the Greek poet Corinna. Lesbia and Lycoris were pseudonyms of real women, but the girls of Tibullus, Propertius, and Ovid are literary creations. Propertius's Cynthia is fiery and tempestuous, a force to be reckoned with; but the characters of the others are sketched very lightly. Delia is soft and perhaps a little timid, Nemesis ruinous, Corinna almost a blank. Although the elegists do not emphasize the point, the girl is not respectable: as Paul Veyne puts it, "she is one of those women one does not marry."[15]

In addition to the all-important girl, the cast of erotic elegy includes two principal supporting characters that we can also trace back to comedy and mime: a rival, always richer than the poet, and a female go-between called a *lena*.[16] The rival is often the girl's current protector, in which case he is called her "husband" (*vir* or *coniunx*). This is the situation Tibullus imagines in *Elegy* 1.2, in which he urges Delia to elude those watching over her

---

13. See James 21–22, 35–41, with earlier bibliography.

14. Lycoreus as a cult title for Apollo appears in the Hellenistic poets Euphorion (fr. 80.3 Powell) and Callimachus (*Hymn* 2.19).

15. Veyne 88.

16. James 41–68.

and slip out of the house for a rendezvous. In *Elegy* 1.6 he urges her "husband" to be more alert; Delia is betraying both of them with a third party (*Elegy* 1.6.15–16):

> But you, heedless husband of a deceiving girl,
> Watch out for me, too, lest she stray.

The "husband's" position, like Tibullus's, is inherently shaky. In *Elegy* 1.5 Tibullus has been supplanted by a rich lover, but things may already be about to change (*Elegy* 1.5.69–76):

> But you, who now feel so sure, be wary of my lot.
> Fickle Fors turns on a nimble wheel.
> Someone even now, and not in vain, stands in the doorway,
> Eagerly looks here and there, makes to withdraw.
> He pretends to be going home. Then before you know it
> There he is at the very door, alone, clearing his throat.
> Secret love ever plots. Be advised: take pleasure while you may.
> Your skiff is swimming over calm water's sway.

The *lena* ("bawd") acts as the girl's agent, advisor, and go-between. She represents the girl's economic interests, usually promoting the claims of the rich rival at the poet's expense, as Tibullus complains in *Elegy* 1.5.47–48:[17]

> This has brought me harm: her rich lover is at home
> And the crafty bawd has occasioned my ruin.

He goes on to load the *lena* with extravagant mouth-filling curses for another ten lines. In *Elegy* 1.6, however, he sees her in a different light—this time she is on his side. He does not call her a *lena* in this poem (the elegists reserve the word for pejorative use); but she plays the part just the same. This time the go-between is none other than Delia's own mother, and the lover reminds Delia of her kindly services (*Elegy* 1.6.57–64):

> Your ancient mother's
> Golden self touches me and soothes my wrath.
> She leads you to me in the shadows and joins our two hands
> In silent secrecy, quite terrified.
> By night she waits for me, rooted outside in the doorway,
> Knows the sound of my step as I approach from afar.
> Live long, my sweet crone! I would like, were I able, to share
> With you a few of my allotted years.

17. Ovid *Amores* 1.8 and Propertius *Elegy* 4.5 both quote the advice of the *lena* at length.

The girl, the *lena,* the rich rival—these are all stock figures from comedy. The lover, too, has a comic antecedent, the foolish youth smitten with the girl, yet too ineffectual to attain her without massive assistance from other characters. But the elegiac lover retains only a few traits of his comic prototype. He is not just part of an ensemble of stock characters, but the star. He is not so young and not nearly so foolish as the imbecilic youth in comedy, and there is no clever slave to help him. Unlike the comic lover, he has other interests—principally poetry and (especially in the case of Tibullus) choosing the best way to lead his life. We will explore these interests in more detail presently. For now it is enough to say that in spite of its comic elements, elegy is a radically different genre, and the complex character of the elegiac lover constitutes a major part of the difference.

The lover in elegy is besotted with his demanding and faithless girl, but the poetry is really about him—his preoccupations (including but not limited to love), his friends, his perspective on the age. We would make a mistake, however, if we believed that the elegiac lover exactly represents the thoughts and feelings of the elegist. No doubt he has some (perhaps many) points in common with his creator, but we can never know which ones. It is better to see him as a persona (or "mask"—the literal meaning of the word) of the poet than to try to match his character and experience with those of the real Tibullus or Propertius or Ovid. The world he lives in has even less relation to reality. It is almost an alternative universe. It is anchored in Augustan Rome and could exist in no other time or place, but its ties to historical reality are fairly loose. Although it touches on the contemporary world and sometimes refers to it directly, it is a separate space, the elegist's creation.

The elegiac world is a counterpart of another alternative landscape, the pastoral world that Virgil presented in the 40s and 30s in his *Eclogues.* Both worlds are imaginary; both set themselves apart from historical reality, and both are affected and defined by that reality. The two worlds and their genres differ in several ways. In pastoral there are many speakers with different and sometimes competing perspectives (there are roughly sixteen singers in the ten *Eclogues*), whereas elegy is dominated by a single first-person speaker and a single ego, focused on himself and expressing just one perspective: his own.[18] Both worlds are conventional, but each employs a different set of conventions. Virgil's pastoral world features sensitive shepherds, singing matches, and an isolated and sympathetic landscape. The

18. Only Propertius gives an entire poem to a speaker other than his own persona, and only a few times: in Books 1–3, *Elegies* 1.21, 1.22, and 3.12, and in several elegies of Book 4, which is dated between around 21 and 16 B.C.E.

elegiac world includes, in addition to a cast with comic antecedents, a set of attitudes that we might lump together under the rubric "elegiac morality." This morality challenges and sometimes even inverts traditional Roman values. It is based on three related tenets: rejection of the active life in favor of the lover's pursuits, love as a military campaign (*militia amoris*), and love as slavery (*servitium amoris*).[19]

Elite men were expected to be active in the service of Rome in politics or war or both; failure to engage in worthwhile endeavor (*negotium*) was decried as inactivity (*otium*), and devotees of such inactivity were seen as idle or useless. Catullus, himself inactive in public life, had already played with the contrast a generation earlier; but although he describes himself as idle (*otiosus*) in specific situations (*Carm.* 10.2, 50.1), he by no means glorifies idleness as a general condition (*Carm.* 51.13–16):

> Idleness, Catullus, is your problem;
> In idleness you are excited and restless.
> Idleness before now has ruined kings
>   And rich cities.

The elegists, by contrast, choose idleness over activity as a way of life, but using different terms. For them the active life is specifically that of a soldier (*militia*); they describe themselves not with the Catullan adjective *otiosus* (a relatively neutral word that we can translate as both "idle" and "with time on one's hands") but as *iners* or *segnis* or *desidiosus* ("slothful," "worthless," "lazy"), more pejorative terms that can also suggest feebleness or passivity. They often bring this convention together with that of love as a military campaign (*militia amoris*), preferring arduous campaigning on the erotic front to traditional warfare. It is more congenial to their sensibility, but hardly idle, they claim, since it involves hardships of its own. Such hardships are particularly involved in their voluntary slavery (*servitium*) to their girl, whom they call *domina*. The word is correctly translated "mistress," but the elegists use it in a very specific sense: the mistress or owner of a slave. Significantly, Catullus never uses it in this way to refer to his Lesbia.[20] He loves her dearly, but he is not her slave. No elite Roman before the elegists would so abase himself, but the topos is an essential hallmark of the genre.

---

19. For a good introduction, see Lyne, *Latin Love Poets* 65–81. See also Murgatroyd, "*Militia amoris*"; Lyne, "*Servitium amoris*"; Gaisser, "*Amor, rura* and *militia*."

20. He uses *domina* twice in *Carmen* 68, both times in the sense "mistress" or "lady of the house" (68.68, 156). The text and interpretation of both verses are disputed, as is the question whether *domina* refers to Lesbia.

The three elegists play with the conventions of elegiac morality in different ways. In *Elegy* 1.1 Tibullus touches on all three of its tenets. To the career of a soldier with its booty and glory he prefers both a quiet life in the country and devotion (and slavery) to his mistress (*Elegy* 1.1.5–6):

> Let my poverty direct me through a lazy life [*vitam . . . inertem*]
> As long as a steadfast flame gleams upon my hearth.

Messalla can adorn his house with the spoils of victory, but Tibullus is chained to his girl as her watchman or doorkeeper, a position reserved for slaves (*Elegy* 1.1.53–58):

> Messalla, for you it is right to make war on land and sea
>   So that your house display the enemy's spoils.
> But the bonds of a beautiful girl bind me fast,
>   And I sit, a watchman before unyielding doors.
> I care nothing for fame: my Delia, as long as I am with you
>   Slacker [*segnis*] I want them to call me, and a shirk [*iners*].

Love has its own battles, he boasts (*Elegy* 1.1.75): "Here is where I am a good soldier in chief!" Propertius takes a similar position in his *Elegy* 1.6.29–30:

> I was not born suited for glory, not suited for arms:
>   The Fates wanted me to enter this service [*militiam*].

Ovid devotes an entire elegy to the *militia amoris,* not contrasting but equating it with the life of a soldier (*Amores* 1.9.1–2, 46):

> Every lover is a soldier, and Cupid has his own camp;
>   Believe me, Atticus: every lover is a soldier.
> . . . .
>   If a man refuses to be lazy [*desidiosus*], let him love!

But although love is its most conspicuous feature, elegiac morality also functions on two other levels: as a serious counter to the contemporary Augustan ethos and as an assertion of the elegists' identities and aspirations as poets. The essence of elegiac morality is its insistence on privileging private life over public concerns, and the elegists' rejection of the *vita activa* expected of men of their class is to some extent a political statement. But it is by no means a simple statement. Complex and nuanced, the stance varies from poet to poet and poem to poem, and even within individual elegies. By choosing to represent the active life by only one of its elements, warfare (*militia*), the elegists were able to use the convention *militia amoris* to pivot or move in the three dimensions of love, politics, and poetry—often simultaneously. *Militia amoris* makes a neat point of contrast between the lives of the lover and the soldier but also between two kinds of poetry: personal (generally with love as its subject) and public (on military or national themes). It makes a contrast, in other words, between elegy and epic. This contrast, too, has a political dimension, but the lines are not always clear. Both Tibullus and Propertius wrote elegies on national themes; Ovid's *Amores* avoids them.[21] But the contrast is also important as a self-conscious literary statement, for it identifies the elegists as devotees of learned Alexandrian poetry, which traced its pedigree back to Callimachus, the great scholar-poet of third-century Alexandria, and was taken up in Rome by Catullus in the 50s B.C.E. and by Virgil in the 40s and 30s. The ideals of Alexandrian poetics are highly complex, but important among them are an insistence on polish and learned allusion and a preference for elegant small-scale poetry over long epic.[22]

The elegists' most conspicuous use of *militia amoris* as a political or poetic statement (or both at the same time) is in what is called a *recusatio,* or refusal to write epic. Propertius and Ovid both play with it, each in his characteristic manner: Propertius with ostentatious Callimachean references and Ovid with self-conscious wit. In *Elegy* 2.1.39–46 Propertius refuses to turn from love elegies to celebration of Caesar (Augustus):[23]

> Neither would Callimachus thunder from his narrow chest
>> The Phlegraean struggles of Jupiter and Enceladus,
> Nor is my heart suited to tracing Caesar's line back
>> To Phrygian ancestors in harsh verse.
> The sailor tells of winds, the farmer of his bulls;
>> The soldier counts his wounds; the shepherd, sheep.
> But we count battles turning on our narrow bed.
>> Let each waste time at what he's best.

Propertius's position is both political and literary, but Ovid makes a case (if we can call it that) that seems purely literary. In the first poem of the *Amores* he claims that he was actually writing a martial epic when Cupid intervened and turned his epic into an elegy (*Amores* 1.1.1–4):

21. Tibullus celebrates Messalla's triumph in *Elegy* 1.7 and the foundation of Rome in *Elegy* 2.5, but in both he mingles personal statement with public themes. Propertius describes the Temple of Apollo on the Palatine in *Elegy* 2.7 and devotes several elegies of Book 4 to national themes.

22. For a general discussion of Alexandrianism in Roman poetry, see Hutchinson 277–354. For Tibullus, see Cairns, *Tibullus* 1–35.

23. Propertius presents a longer and stronger *recusatio* in *Elegies* 3.1–5, a complex statement of Callimachean principles with highly political overtones.

> I was getting ready to publish arms and savage wars
> > In high verse—the subject suited to the measures.
> The second verse was as long as the first. Cupid laughed
> > And snatched away one of its feet.

Cupid's metrical theft makes Ovid's second line into a pentameter, changing his epic hexameters into elegiac couplets and turning the poet into an elegist. He complains that he has nothing to write about in his new meter (*Amores* 1.1.19–20):

> I have no subject suited to lighter numbers,
> > Not a boy, not a girl with tresses done up in a knot.

Cupid remedies the omission with his arrow, and Ovid accepts his fate (*Amores* 1.1.27–30):

> My work rises in six feet, falls back in five;
> > Farewell, iron wars, along with your measures.
> Bind your blond hair with sea-born myrtle,
> > Muse counted out in eleven-foot lengths.

Tibullus, by contrast, presents no overt *recusatio*. He does not explain what he refuses to write but rather presents what he chooses to write. He uses the same tenets of elegiac morality as his fellow poets, but he keeps his poetics (both Callimachean and political) under the surface of his poems. We will look more closely at his Alexandrianism presently. As for the politics of his poetry, for now it is perhaps enough to say that he celebrates the public achievements of Messalla and his family and that he writes no epics. He leaves these facts and his use of the elegiac conventions to tell us why.

Elegy was useful to its poets on a number of levels. It was an ancient genre that had always allowed for a wide variety of subjects and attitudes, both personal and political. Although ostensibly modest in comparison with the loftier genres of epic and tragedy, it had valuable Alexandrian antecedents: it was the preferred mode of Callimachus. The Callimachean principles of learning, exquisite technique, and minute attention to style had dominated Roman poetry for a generation; elegy with its Alexandrian credentials was well placed to follow in the tradition, but as a fresh genre for a new group of young poets. Most important, however, elegy provided a new space for poetry in Rome after Actium. The world of elegy—private not public, insisting on its own modest position, and floating above political realities like a balloon tied just here and there to the ground—allowed the poets both to stand apart from the new dispensation and to respond to it selectively and on their own terms.

TIBULLUS

The Tibullan corpus as we have it is small: just two short books of Tibullus's own poetry, together with a group of poems by other authors that were added at some point in antiquity. Of this group only the elegies and epigrams of Lygdamus and Sulpicia are included in the present volume. The entire collection fills only 75 pages in the Oxford Classical Text. (The elegies of Tibullus himself take up just 46.) Propertius's four books, by contrast, fill around 190 pages; the three books of Ovid's *Amores,* 100. Tibullus's writing career was short, only about a decade or so at most, between Actium and his death around 19; but that fact alone cannot account for his slender production. The nature of his art was undoubtedly also a factor. Tibullus was an extraordinarily careful and fastidious poet who paid meticulous attention to the artistic nuance of every word—a point that emerges from close reading of the elegies and one abundantly demonstrated by the literary-critical studies of modern scholars.[24] Minute care on the level shown by the elegies is inherently time-consuming—and in the best tradition of Roman Alexandrianism, which placed a high value on what we could call "slow poetry."[25] Tibullus's own temperament and intentions must also have played a role, but here we have no hard biographical or stylistic evidence, only an impression (one can put it no more strongly than that) drawn from the elegies themselves. Tibullus presents himself (whether frankly or somewhat disingenuously we cannot be sure) as a poet writing to suit himself and a small (perhaps very small) group of friends rather than as one seeking to establish himself with a wide audience. Propertius and Ovid present themselves as looking for readers and fame and keep themselves in the public eye with dozens of poems. Tibullus, not claiming these ambitions, could afford a more leisurely timetable.

Ovid tells us that Tibullus is the earliest of the surviving Augustan elegists (*Tristia* 4.10.51–54):[26]

24. See especially Putnam, "Simple Tibullus" and "Virgil and Tibullus"; Cairns, *Tibullus;* Miller, *Subjecting Verses* 95–129.

25. Catullus (*Carmen* 95) praised Cinna for taking nine years to write the *Zmyrna.* Only a few fragments of Cinna's poem are preserved, but it was probably no longer than 500 or 600 lines.

26. Ovid presents the elegists in the same order in *Tristia* 2.445–68.

Virgil I only saw, nor did the mean Fates grant
   Tibullus time for my friendship.
He was your successor, Gallus; Propertius came next,
   And after these I was the fourth in the series.

Most scholars have disagreed, awarding priority to Propertius, but the question has been reopened in an important recent article supporting Ovid's chronology.[27] Debate will surely continue, but the important point for the present discussion is that both Tibullus and Propertius were writing elegies very soon after Actium—in both cases as early as 30/29.[28] Individual elegies of both undoubtedly circulated soon after their composition, and we can be sure that the two poets read and responded to each other's work. The close correspondence in thought noted earlier between Tibullus's *Elegy* 1.1 and Propertius's *Elegy* 1.6 is a good example of such a response. (Scholars will disagree about which poet started the dialogue.)

At some point in the early 20s Tibullus gathered ten of his elegies and issued them as a book. A second book of six poems, perhaps cut short by his death, was issued around 19 or so. The two books treat similar subjects (love, Messalla, the joys of a quiet life in the country), but they differ in important details, and especially in tone. The second is much darker, as we will see presently. Tibullus's variety of subjects immediately distinguishes him from the other elegists, especially from the Propertius of Books 1 and 2, with his nearly single-minded focus on love. But love is only one of Tibullus's major themes—and not just one love, at that. In Book 1 he celebrates both Delia and the boy Marathus; in Book 2, a cruel girl called Nemesis. Propertius, by contrast, loves only his Cynthia. As he says at the end of *Elegy* 1.12 (verses 19–20):

   It is not right for me to love another or to stop loving her.
   Cynthia was the beginning; Cynthia will be the end.

In publishing his first book as a collection of ten Tibullus was following a model established by Horace's first book of *Satires* and Virgil's *Eclogues* in the previous decade: a carefully articulated collection so patterned that its whole would have greater meaning than the sum of its parts. Virgil is the

27. Knox 204–16. The only datable event in Tibullus's first book is the triumph Messalla celebrated in 27 for his victories in Gaul (*Elegy* 1.7). Knox dates Messalla's campaign to 30 or 29 and argues that Tibullus is anticipating rather than describing the triumph of 27.

28. Lyne, "Propertius and Tibullus" 521, dates the events of Propertius *Elegy* 1.6 to the year 30.

closer model—framing his varied themes in a remote world both imaginary and yet somehow touched by historical reality, celebrating and lamenting both homosexual and heterosexual love, creating a symmetrical structure that is both unmistakable and yet resistant to diagram. Tibullus works in a similar way in Book 1. *Elegies* 1.1 and 1.10 are the frame, setting Tibullus's longing for life in the country and the pleasures of love against the claims and demands of war. But the symmetry is not absolute. In *Elegy* 1.1 Tibullus rejects war for life in the countryside; in 1.10 he is being dragged off to battle and prays to the Lares, his ancient household gods, to protect him. The elegy ends with an appeal to Peace (*Pax*), who is not just an abstract idea but a goddess (*Elegy* 1.10.67–68):

> But, kindly Pax, come here to us. Grasp the corn stalk.
> May your bright bosom brim with fruit, where'er you walk.

The book revolves around Tibullus's lovers Delia and Marathus, or it may be better to say that it moves from the one to the other: Delia figures in *Elegies* 1.1, 1.2, 1.3, 1.5, and 1.6; Marathus interrupts the Delia sequence in 1.4 and reappears in 1.8 and 1.9. The two sequences suggest rather than tell stories, each moving from hope of attaining the lover (*Elegies* 1.1–4) to despair and disdain (*Elegies* 1.5, 1.6, 1.8, and 1.9). The Marathus sequence comes to a harsher end than the Delia. In *Elegy* 1.6 (the last Delia elegy) Tibullus reminds Delia of the pain and poverty awaiting an unfaithful woman in old age but withdraws the threat at the last minute (*Elegy* 1.6.83–86):

> Aloft on high Olympus Venus observes her in tears,
> And warns the fickle just how pitiless she is prone.
> Let these curses fall elsewhere, Delia. Let us each be
> A model of love as our hair grows white to see.

In the corresponding Marathus elegy (1.9), Tibullus gloats that Marathus is going to get his comeuppance and promises a thank offering to Venus (*Elegy* 1.9.81–84):

> Then may your punishment delight me, and a golden palm affixed
> To my saving Venus may mark my fate:
> *Tibullus, released from a false love, offers this, Goddess, to you.*
> *He asks that your kindly thoughts toward him be true.*

But it is Tibullus's friend Messalla who holds the book together. He is prominently and affectionately invoked in *Elegies* 1.1, 1.3, 1.5, and 1.7, and Tibullus uses him to represent not only the soldier's life he rejects for himself but also the glory and greatness of that life. *Elegy* 1.7, though numerically slightly off center, is the centerpiece of the book. It provides a break between Delia and Marathus. (Or perhaps we should say a break between the breakups with Delia and Marathus, since Marathus appears in 1.4.) But its quasi-central position has another and more important function: to evoke the public world of war and politics in a personal way at the heart of the book. A tribute to Messalla as both general and friend, the elegy celebrates his great public achievement, the triumph, in the context of his private birthday festivity. Here again Virgil was probably the model, for he too evoked historical reality near the center of his book. *Eclogues* 4 and 5 sing of the hopes and fears of the triumviral period, transforming real events into pastoral visions, just as Tibullus celebrates an Augustan victory (although he does not call it that) by bringing it into the private world of elegy.

The second book also shows signs of artful arrangement, whether by Tibullus himself or by a sensitive editor after his death.[29] Its six elegies fall into two groups that are different in genre, subject, and tone. *Elegies* 2.1, 2.2, and 2.5 are what we might call ceremonial narratives, in which Tibullus officiates almost like a priest, both directing and describing ritual or festive events. The poems treat a cluster of closely associated themes: the land, Messalla and his family and associates, early Rome. Their tone is one of affectionate reverence to land, friends, and ritual alike. *Elegies* 2.3, 2.4, and 2.6 are dramatic monologues on Tibullus's affair with Nemesis. Their tone is dark—much darker than the tone in the elegies to Delia and Marathus in Book 1—and the mood becomes increasingly bleak in the course of the sequence. Nemesis is cruel and unattainable. She cares only for gifts, and Tibullus is so obsessed with her that he is willing not only to undergo the usual *servitium amoris,* but even to suffer the degradation of losing his ancestral lands to satisfy her greed (*Elegy* 2.4.52–54):

> Our Amor must be worshipped according to her rules.
> Even if her order says sell the ancestral estate,
>   Lares, submit to her will and her command.

Tibullus bridges the gap between his two disparate groups by placing their elegies in an interlocking order: the sequence of ceremonial narratives is interrupted by *Elegies* 2.3 and 2.4 on Nemesis and resumes with *Elegy* 2.5; the book ends with a final Nemesis poem, *Elegy* 2.6. He also places small connectors between the groups within individual poems. *Elegy* 2.2 is a

29. Murgatroyd, *Tibullus: Elegies II* xi–xv; Maltby 52–53.

ceremonial narrative, *Elegy* 2.3 a dramatic monologue on Nemesis; Tibullus addresses both to Cornutus. Near the end of the ceremonial elegy 2.5 Nemesis makes a cameo appearance (2.5.109–18) that leads into the erotic elegy 2.6.

Tibullus's lovers come and go: in Book 1 Delia and Marathus; in Book 2, Nemesis. But Messalla is the essential constant throughout, although he seems more remote in Book 2—now less the subject of direct address than of oblique and respectful reference. He is invoked only in the ceremonial narratives. In *Elegy* 2.1 Tibullus addresses him as if he were a god, toasting him in his absence and looking to him for inspiration for his hymn of thanksgiving to the rural gods (*Elegy* 2.1.31–36):

> But *Here's to Messalla!* may each and every one say to his cups.
> Let every word reecho the name of him away.
> Messalla, famed for your triumph over the Aquitani,
> Conqueror, glory of your unshorn forebears,
> Be present here, and lend me your spirit while we render
> Thanks to the farmers' deities with our song.

In *Elegy* 2.2 Messalla is evoked only indirectly, through the celebration of the birthday and marriage of his friend (and perhaps kinsman) Cornutus.[30] In *Elegy* 2.5 Tibullus celebrates the induction of Messalla's son Messallinus into the priestly college in charge of the Sibylline Books in 21 B.C.E.[31] Messalla himself is named only at the end of the elegy, when Tibullus, predicting a future triumph for the young Messallinus, imagines Messalla proudly witnessing the event (*Elegy* 2.5.119–20):

> Then let my Messalla sponsor entertainment for the crowd,
> And, as father, applaud when the chariot passes by.

Both books of the *Elegies* show Tibullus as a consummate craftsman deeply steeped in both the subjects and the techniques of Greek and Roman Alexandrian poetry. Unlike his Alexandrian predecessors and contemporaries, however, he displays no interest in what we might almost consider the distinguishing feature of Alexandrian poetics: claiming a place in the poetic tradition. All the other Alexandrians, from Callimachus on through Catullus, Virgil, Horace, and the other Augustan elegists, present themselves in an artistic continuum—sometimes praising or blaming fellow poets, sometimes claiming artistic descent from great predecessors.

---

30. Cairns, "Tibullus 2.2," esp. 227–31.
31. Marcus Valerius Messalla Messallinus.

Propertius calls himself the Roman Callimachus (*Elegy* 4.1.64); Ovid lists his place in the succession of elegists (*Tristia* 4.10.51–54). Tibullus alone never mentions the name of another poet.[32]

The boy Marathus is Tibullus's most obvious Alexandrian subject; coy and venal, he has numerous antecedents in Hellenistic epigrams and especially in the *Iambi* of Callimachus.[33] The themes associated with Marathus also have Alexandrian parallels. In *Elegy* 1.4 Tibullus receives instruction about how to win him from a speaking statue of Priapus (an Alexandrian motif).[34] In *Elegy* 1.8 Tibullus poses as the instructor and urges the girl Pholoe to accommodate Marathus. The scene is worthy of Hellenistic iambus or mime, as is that in *Elegy* 1.9, where Tibullus complains that his boy has defected to a disgusting old man for the sake of gifts.[35]

Tibullus's poetic techniques are Alexandrian at almost every level.[36] Here we can consider only a few examples. In *Elegy* 1.7 he enhances his celebration of Messalla's birthday and triumph with echoes from Callimachus, Ennius, and Catullus, placing them in the text almost like birthday surprises to add to Messalla's enjoyment of the poem.[37] Messalla was a highly cultivated man with a connoisseur's knowledge of Greek and Latin poetry. Spotting the allusions would have amused him, but that would have been only part of the game; when he identified the source and context of each one, he would see a witty compliment, for each celebrates a great athletic, military, or mythological hero. The quotations from Callimachus come from poems celebrating the athletic victories of Sosibius, the minister of Ptolemy IV; the echo of Ennius, from a passage leading up to the military victory of the Roman admiral Lucius Aemilius Regillus; and the echo of Catullus, from the song of the Parcae predicting the feats of Achilles in Catullus's *Carmen* 64.[38]

Tibullus can also use allusion to shape an entire poem. In *Elegy* 1.3.3–4 he is alone and sick far from home on the island of Corcyra, which he calls

---

32. The only exception would be at *Elegy* 1.10.11, if we accept the emendation *Valgi* for *vulgi* transmitted by the manuscripts. Valgius was a poet (see Glossary), but the passage makes no reference to poetry.

33. Maltby 45–46, 58–59,60–61; Dawson.

34. Maltby 215–16.

35. For parallels between *Elegy* 1.9 and Callimachus *Iambus* 3, see Dawson 1–15.

36. For a detailed discussion, see Cairns, *Tibullus*. See also Bulloch.

37. For *Elegy* 1.7, see Gaisser, "Tibullus 1.7."

38. Tibullus *Elegy* 1.7. 22, 23: cf. Callimachus fr. 384.27, 31–32 Pf. *Elegy* 1.7.28: cf. Callimachus fr. 383.16 Pf. *Elegy* 1.7.12: cf. Ennius *Annales* 384–85. *Elegy* 1.7.1: cf. Cat. 64.383.

by the Homeric name Phaeacia—a learned identification seemingly also made by Callimachus:[39]

> Sick, in the clasp of Phaeacia's unknown land, I pray:
> Black Mors, unclasp your grasping hands.

With the single word *Phaeacia* Tibullus brings us into an elegiac *Odyssey* with himself as the stranded Odysseus and Delia as a most improbable Penelope. Odysseus paid a visit to Hades (*Odyssey* 11). Tibullus pictures himself in an elegiac Underworld where Elysium is populated by lovers and Tartarus by those guilty of crimes against love, including his rivals for Delia (*Elegy* 1.3.57–82). The poem ends with a prayer to Delia to be faithful until his safe return (*Elegy* 1.3.83–94):

> But, I beseech you, keep chaste, and may your attentive nurse
>   Stay by you always to guard your modesty.
> Let her tell you stories, and when the lamp is lit,
>   Let her guide down long strands from full distaff,
> While bit by bit the servant girl, intent upon her weighty work,
>   Grows drowsy, then slips slowly off to sleep.
> Then may I suddenly arrive, with no warning ahead.
>   May my presence seem to you sent from heaven above.
> And, just as you are, Delia, long hair all tangled
>   And feet bare, hurry and run to me.
> May Aurora then bring us this Lucifer—this I pray—
>   Brilliant with roseate steeds, on that bright day.

The picture of Delia spinning identifies her as chaste, for spinning was seen as a typical activity of virtuous women, whether they were honorable Roman matrons ("she made wool" is a frequent phrase in epitaphs) or faithful mistresses in comedy and elegy.[40] But the scene also evokes Penelope's famous weaving and her joyous recognition of the returned Odysseus.[41]

---

39. Callimachus *Aetia* fr. 15 Pf.; and see Maltby 185–86.

40. For some examples of woolworking as a detail in Roman epitaphs, see Lattimore 297–98. Livy, writing at about the same time as Tibullus, demonstrates the virtue of Lucretia by describing her as spinning by lamplight (*History of Rome* 1.57.9). A close parallel to the scene in Tibullus is found in Terence's comedy *The Self-Tormentor* 275–307. Propertius's Cynthia claims to have kept herself awake by spinning as she waited for Propertius (Propertius *Elegy* 1.3.41).

41. For Penelope's joy, see *Odyssey* 23.207–8: "she burst into tears and ran straight to him, throwing / her arms around the neck of Odysseus, and kissed his head" (trans. Richmond Lattimore).

With Aurora and her "roseate steeds" (*Elegy* 1.3.93–94), which recall the famous Homeric phrase "rosy-fingered Dawn," Tibullus brings his *Odyssey* to a close.

Tibullus's learned care is also evident on a smaller scale, in individual words and phrases. It appears in his sound patterning and word order, but above all in his extensive use of etymological wordplay, which has been defined as "explicit reference or implicit allusion to the etymology of one of the words a poet is using."[42] These etymologies, often shown by modern scholars to be incorrect, had a high intellectual standing in antiquity. Wordplay of this kind is as old as Homer, but it was brought to a new level by the Greek Alexandrians, scholars as well as poets, who used it especially in their aetiologies linking past myths and events with present cults and institutions. Tibullus's most famous use of it is in *Elegy* 2.5, his longest and most ambitious poem.[43] The elegy celebrates Messallinus's induction as one of the priests in charge of the Sibylline Books, which were kept in the new Temple of Apollo on the Palatine Hill. Messallinus appears at the beginning and the end of the poem, but the long central portion treats the foundation and destiny of Rome. Framing this central portion are the passages in which Tibullus has concentrated his etymological wordplay: two accounts of the rustic festival of the Parilia, feast of the shepherds' goddess Pales, which was celebrated on April 21, the anniversary of the city's founding. The first celebration (not explicitly identified as the Parilia) occurs on the Palatine in the remote past before Romulus's foundation of the city (*Elegy* 2.5.23–38). The second takes place in the countryside in the present, as an indication of peace restored after the evil days of civil strife (*Elegy* 2.5.83–104). Both passages play on the root *pa-*, as in "*pa*sture" and "*pa*stor" (shepherd).

The first Parilia, on the early Palatine (*Elegy* 2.5.25–30):

> At that time cows cropped [*pascebant*] the grassy Palatium
> And lowly huts stood on Jove's citadel.
> Pan, dripping with milk, took shade there under an oak,
> And a wooden Pales was fashioned with rustic hook,
> And the chattering pipe, sacred to the sylvan god, was hanging
> On a tree, a wandering shepherd's [*pastoris*] offering.

The second Parilia, in the countryside (*Elegy* 2.5.87–88):

---

42. O'Hara 2–3.

43. Cairns, *Tibullus* 80–82. For an account showing the prevalence of etymologies in Tibullus, see Cairns, "Ancient 'Etymology.'"

And the shepherd [*pastor*], steeped in Bacchus, will sing the festive
 Parilia.

The second description of the Parilia, which emphasizes the fertility of
crops and women, implies (but does not explicitly refer to) another impor-
tant *pa-* etymology: *parere,* "produce," "give birth."

These etymologies are not mere wordplay, although they were no doubt
meant to be savored and enjoyed by the reader. They underline a serious
point that Tibullus makes over and over again in his poetry: the value of
rustic simplicity and the worship of the old country gods. By framing the
central section on the Roman destiny with the highly charged visions of
fertility, piety, and a simple life underlined in the etymological complex
Palatium, pascebant, Pan, Pales, pastor, Parilia (and the implied *parere*), he
brings past and present together and suggests that the ancient values are
fundamental to Rome itself.

Many of the themes of *Elegy* 2.5 were current in the late 20s—in the
poetry of Tibullus's contemporaries, in art, and in Augustan ideology.
Tibullus opens the elegy with a prayer to Apollo in his temple on the
Palatine (*Elegy* 2.5.1–10):

Phoebus, bless us. A new priest enters your temple.
 Come to us, here and now, with lyre and song.
Now strike the melodious strings with your thumb, I pray:
 Now turn my words to the tunes of praise.
And with your brow bound with a triumph's laurel,
 While they heap your altars, come, yourself, to your rites.
But come, shimmering and beautiful. Don, now, this raiment
 Long set aside. Now comb well your streaming locks,
As in that time when, after King Saturn's rout,
 They recall you sang out the glory of conquering Jove.

Apollo was Octavian's patron deity. The temple itself, which Octavian had
vowed after his defeat of Sextus Pompey in 36, was built next to his house
on the Palatine and dedicated in 28. It contained two statues of Apollo with
his lyre. Tibullus's description of the god probably alludes to the statue of
Apollo Citharoedus by the fourth-century sculptor Scopas, for it was under
the pedestal of this statue that the Sibylline Books were kept.[44] The temple
is mentioned by both Horace and Propertius (Horace *Odes* 1.31; Propertius
Elegies 2.31, 4.6).

---

44. For Apollo and Octavian (Augustus), see Zanker 49–53; for the temple, see
85–89.

The picture of primeval Rome at Tibullus's *Elegy* 2.5.23–38 has parallels in both Virgil and Propertius.[45] In these cases, as in Tibullus, an essential point of the description is to contrast the primitive site of the city with its present aspect. Here is Tibullus in *Elegy* 2.5.55–56 (the speaker is the prophesying Sibyl):

> Now while you may, bulls, feed on the grass of the Seven Hills.
> Presently a great city will arise here.

Descriptions of early Rome were nothing new; they had been a favorite topic of Roman antiquarians in the previous generation.[46] But they came to prominence in the 20s, largely as a consequence of Augustus's ambitious building program, which dramatically changed the aspect of the city and invited comparison with its simpler past.[47]

The Sibyl's prophecy about the foundation of Rome (*Elegy* 2.5.39–64) is reminiscent of similar prophecies in the *Aeneid*, but it is unnecessary to claim direct influence, since the general outlines of the Aeneas legend were well established. The more important point is that the story was of current interest in the 20s and that poets could handle it in different ways. The closest parallel to the prophecy in *Elegy* 2.5, which the Sibyl gives directly to Aeneas himself, is Jupiter's prophecy to Venus in *Aeneid* 1.257–96. Both prophecies guarantee Aeneas and the Trojans a home in Latium and victory over the Rutulians. Both prophesy Aeneas's divinity, Ascanius's foundation of Alba Longa, and the birth of Romulus and Remus; and both include a grand vision of empire. In the *Aeneid* Jupiter says of Romulus's Romans (*Aeneid* 1.278–79):

> I place no boundary of space or time on their achievement.
> I have given them empire without end.

Here is Tibullus's Sibyl (*Elegy* 2.5.57–60):

> Rome, your name strikes awe in the countries you will rule,
>   Where Ceres gazes down from heaven upon her fields,
> Where Sol's risings open, and where the Ocean stream washes
>   His breathless horses in its rushing waves.

In Virgil the link between the Julian line and that of Aeneas and Ascanius (Iulus) is explicit (*Aeneid* 1.286–88):

---

45. Virgil *Aeneid* 8.314–61. Propertius *Elegies* 4.1.1–38, 4.2.1–10, 4.4.1–14, 4.9.
46. White 184–85.
47. White 185–90.

A Trojan Caesar will be born of glorious pedigree,
Who will bound his empire with Ocean, his glory with the stars,
Iulius, a name handed down from great Iulus.

Tibullus draws the connection more obliquely—not in a prophecy of Julian glory but with a list of the awful omens after Caesar's assassination (*Elegy* 2.5.71–78).[48]

The themes that we have looked at in *Elegy* 2.5 are generally described as Augustan, as are various ideas that Tibullus uses throughout his poetry: the virtues of simple country life, celebration of traditional festivals, family life, and the continuity of the generations.[49] All these ideas were important in Augustan ideology. But scholars have often suggested that Tibullus was somehow opposed or resistant to the Augustan regime. The argument is usually based on two points: the fact that Tibullus never mentions the name of Augustus, and the idea that he was deferring to the political views of Messalla, who has often been characterized as either anti-Augustan or at least independent in his ideas. But the perception about Messalla's position is incorrect. Both Messalla and his sons were well placed in the Augustan establishment.[50] Messalla was consul with Octavian in 31. After Actium he was awarded joint possession with Agrippa of Antony's house on the Palatine. He was given a triumph in 27, and he enjoyed other honors in the 20s, including election to the ancient and highly prestigious priesthood of the Arval Brethren, recently revived by Augustus.[51] Messallinus was chosen as one of the priests in charge of the Sibylline Books and went on to celebrate a triumph of his own in 11 C.E. In omitting the name of Augustus, then, Tibullus was not deferring to the political stance of Messalla, but perhaps he was still respecting his wishes. Great aristocrats like Messalla befriended poets not in order to have them celebrate others (not even Augustus) but to publicize themselves and secure their own place in history.[52] In employing Augustan themes Tibullus was able to celebrate Messalla by association, since he was so well placed in the regime. At the same time he was able to

48. "Suddenly we are in the year 44 witnessing the portents that followed upon the death of Julius Caesar (described at greater length by Vergil at *Georg.* 1.464–88)" (Putnam, *Tibullus* 191).

49. For the continuity of generations, see especially *Elegies* 1.7.55–56; 1.10.39–42, 47–48; 2.2.21–22; 2.5.91–94.

50. White 40; Butrica.

51. Cairns, *Tibullus* 132.

52. Butrica 293–95. "Messalla, it seems, felt no compulsion to share the glory of Tibullus' poetry, and Augustus felt no need to intrude" (p. 295).

draw on a complex of ideas that was rich in artistic possibilities for every poet of his generation.

LYGDAMUS AND SULPICIA

Tibullus's elegies have come down to us together with a number of poems by other authors. The Tibullan corpus contains Books 1 and 2 of Tibullus, six elegies by Lygdamus, the *Panegyric of Messalla* (a long poem in hexameters praising Messalla), the *Garland of Sulpicia* (a group of five epigrams on the love affair of Sulpicia and Cerinthus), six epigrams by Sulpicia herself, and an elegy and epigram falsely purporting to be by Tibullus. The collection was put together at an unknown date, but almost certainly by around 350 C.E.[53] Originally it consisted of three books (the two by Tibullus and a third with the work of the other poets), but at some point in the fifteenth century, scribes divided the third book into two, beginning a fourth book with the *Panegyric of Messalla*. Since some editors follow the original division into three books and others the later division into four, it is conventional to supply both sets of numbers for the poems of the fourth book. Thus, Sulpicia's poems are numbered 3.13–18 (= 4.7–12).

At least five or six different poets seem to be represented in the Tibullan corpus. Of these, three are associated with Messalla: Tibullus, Sulpicia (Messalla's niece and ward), and the anonymous poet of the *Panegyric of Messalla*. Tibullus and Sulpicia were members of the circle of Messalla; the personal relation, if any, between Messalla and the poet of the panegyric is unknown. The connection of these poets with Messalla has led scholars to believe that the collection as a whole is to be associated with him and that all the poets were members of his circle. From this idea it is only a small step to the suggestion that an ancient editor found the various poems in the family archives of Messalla and assembled them into our present collection.[54] The idea, as attractive as it is, has been disputed by recent scholars, some of whom would date both Lygdamus and even the *Panegyric of Messalla* to the end of the first century C.E.[55] The jury on the question is still out.

The identity of Lygdamus is unknown. His name appears only once in his elegies—in the epitaph he imagines for his tomb (Lygdamus 2.29–30):

53. Navarro Antolín 29–30.
54. Smith 87; Luck, *Latin Love Elegy* 102.
55. Tränkle 1–6, 55–63, 173–84; Navarro Antolín 16–20, 25–30.

> *Here Lygdamus lies. His cause of death was grief,*
> *Of his wife, Neaera, painfully bereft.*

His poems contain only one clue about his life. In his fifth elegy Lygdamus describes himself as a young man (Lygdamus 5.15–16) and goes on to give the year of his birth (5.17–18):

> My parents first beheld my hour of birth the day
> When each consul fell by one and the same fate.

At first sight the couplet suggests that Lygdamus was born in 43, the year in which the consuls Hirtius and Pansa both fell at the battle of Mutina. But the clue creates more problems than it solves, for Ovid gives his own date of birth in exactly the same words (*Tristia* 4.10.6). It is possible that both poets were born in 43 B.C.E., but it is very unlikely that they would have chosen the same words to say so unless one was imitating the other. If Lygdamus is the imitator, we would have to date his poem after the publication of the *Tristia* (that is, after 11 or 12 C.E.); if he was born in 43, that would make him fifty-five or fifty-six years old when he wrote the elegy, hardly the young man he claims to be in lines 15–16. There are only two answers to the conundrum that would square with both Lygdamus's claim of youth and a birth year in which two consuls fell. The first possible answer is that Ovid is the imitator and that both poets were born in 43. The second is that Lygdamus is the imitator but he is dating his birth not to 43 but rather to another year when two consuls perished: 69 C.E., when the consuls Servius Sulpicius Galba and Titus Vinnius were assassinated.[56] To put it another way, Lygdamus is to be dated either to the Augustan period or to that of the Flavians, over a century later. There is as yet no scholarly consensus on the matter.

Lygdamus has a major point in common with the other elegists: his preoccupation with love. He celebrates Neaera, a cruel and faithless mistress cut from the same piece of cloth as Tibullus's Delia and Nemesis, Propertius's Cynthia, and Ovid's Corinna. Neaera is the subject of five of his six elegies; in the remaining poem, he treats another favorite elegiac subject, his sickness and dread of death (Lygdamus 5).

But Lygdamus's differences from the other elegists are as conspicuous as his similarities to them. Like the rest, Lygdamus uses a pseudonym for his mistress, but, unlike the rest, he also uses one for himself—a striking departure. He has chosen a name that identifies him as a slave (Propertius's

---

56. Navarro Antolín 18–19, with earlier bibliography.

Cynthia had a slave called Lygdamus, and the name is attested in inscriptions); but of course he is not a real slave, only a slave of love in the usual *servitium amoris.*[57] The pseudonym was perhaps intended to invite speculation about his real identity; and modern scholars have accepted the invitation, trying (in vain) to identify him with everyone from Tibullus and the young Ovid to Ovid's brother, one of Messalla's sons, and even Cynthia's slave Lygdamus.[58] But the important point is simply the pseudonym itself: Lygdamus, whoever he was, differed from his fellow elegists (and other Roman poets) in seeking anonymity rather than fame.

His elegies do not sketch the usual elegiac story that moves from happiness to disillusionment, despair, and ultimate separation. There are no happy moments in Lygdamus: he is separated from Neaera from first to last. The familiar elegiac conventions are missing. Apart from a brief reference to the *servitium amoris* in Lygdamus 4.65–74, there is no hint of elegiac morality: no *militia amoris,* no justification of the lover's avoidance of the *vita activa,* no argument for writing on love rather than war. Even the usual elegiac cast of characters is strangely reduced: there is no *lena,* and even the rival is barely in evidence. He appears only indirectly, when Apollo appears to Lygdamus in a dream to announce that Neaera is unfaithful (4.57–58):

> Neaera the beautiful, extolled through your songs,
> Prefers to be the girl of another man.

In the lines quoted above Lygdamus uses the usual elegiac terminology in which the poet calls his mistress *puella* ("girl") and her protector *vir* ("man" or "husband"). But elsewhere he deviates from the standard pattern, using the language of marriage for himself and Neaera. He calls their relationship "marriage"(*coniugium*), himself "husband" (*vir*), and Neaera "wife" (*coniunx*)—terms never used in this sense by the other elegists of themselves and their mistresses.[59] In the other elegists the terminology of marriage is used for the girl and her protector, not for the girl and the poet.

Lygdamus's elegiac world is different from that of the other elegists: in its lack of the standard conventions, in its reduced cast of characters, and in its terminology for the lovers. But it differs in another major respect as well: it

57. For Cynthia's Lygdamus, see Propertius *Elegies* 3.6.2, 4.7.35.
58. For these and other identifications, see Navarro Antolín 7–15.
59. *Coniugium:* Lygdamus 2.4.74, 2.4.79; *vir,* of Lygdamus in relation to Neaera: Lygdamus 1.23, 2.14; of any lover in relation to his girl: Lygdamus 4.52, 4.62; *coniunx,* of Neaera in relation to Lygdamus: Lygdamus 1.26, 1.27, 2.30, 3.32; of any girl in relation to her lover: Lygdamus 2.4.

contains no reference to historical reality. Its only characters are Lygdamus and Neaera and a few unnamed friends. Everything in it is a fiction, including the name of the poet himself. But reality was essential to the other elegists: the world of their poetry was a space anchored, however loosely, to contemporary Rome and providing both an alternative and a response to it. Lygdamus's world, by contrast, is neither affected nor defined by anything outside itself.

The Tibullan corpus contains two groups of poems associated with Sulpicia. The poems of the first group, often called the *Garland of Sulpicia,* are the work of an anonymous poet of uncertain date who writes about the love affair of Sulpicia and Cerinthus, sometimes as a friendly observer and sometimes in the voice of Sulpicia (3.8–12 = 4.2–6). The poems of the second group, translated in this volume, are the work of Sulpicia herself (3.13–18 = 4.7–12).[60]

Sulpicia is a remarkable figure in Roman literary history, for she is the only woman of the classical period writing in Latin whose works have survived.[61] We are fortunate in knowing something about her, although not nearly enough to give a full portrait. Apart from Tibullus himself, she is the only poet in the Tibullan corpus who can be identified. Like Lygdamus, she mentions her name only once, but unlike Lygdamus, she is very specific. She is "Servius's daughter, Sulpicia" (Sulpicia 4.4). In Sulpicia 2.5 she calls Messalla "kinsman." The two references tell us exactly who she is: the daughter of Servius Sulpicius Rufus, who was married to Messalla's sister Valeria. Her pedigree on both sides is socially and intellectually impeccable. The importance of her connection with Messalla is obvious, but her father's family were also highly cultivated Roman aristocrats. Her father was a distinguished orator; her grandfather, another Servius Sulpicius Rufus (consul in 51), had been a famous legal scholar.[62]

Sulpicia's extant work consists of six epigrams totaling just forty lines in all. Like the elegists, she writes about love, and like them she uses a pseudonym for her lover. She calls him Cerinthus but tells us almost nothing about him. His character and identity remain as shadowy as those of any elegiac *puella,* and he is named only twice in the epigrams (Sulpicia 2.2, 5.1). The epigrams are very artfully ordered, whether by Sulpicia herself or by a later editor. They are arranged not to tell a story but to move from public to private revelation.

60. The following studies of Sulpicia are highly recommended: Santirocco; Lowe; Hinds; Flaschenriem.
61. But we do have two verses by another Sulpicia, a satirist of the age of Domitian.
62. Syme, "A Great Orator Mislaid."

In the first epigram Sulpicia proclaims to the world that she and her lover have consummated their love. The poem is programmatic, announcing not only that the speaker is a woman but that everything that follows will be colored by the fact of the sexual relationship proclaimed at the beginning. In the last epigram she addresses only her lover, confessing that she had left him the night before in order to avoid confessing the extent of her passion (Sulpicia 6.5–6):

> ... last night I left you all alone
> In my desire to mask my burning flame.

Epigrams 2 and 3 are a pair: in 2 Sulpicia complains that Messalla is taking her to the country so that she cannot spend her birthday with Cerinthus; in 3 she will be able to stay in the city after all. In epigram 4 she scornfully castigates her lover for unfaithfulness, and in 5 she worries that he is not concerned enough that she is sick.

Sulpicia's epigrams are short (the longest has ten lines), but they are anything but simple. She packs a lot of ideas into a small space, often articulating the complicated connections between them in an equally complicated syntax. Here is the first couplet of her opening poem (Sulpicia 1.1–2):

> At last a love has come such that repute of having hid it
> Would shame me more than had I laid it bare.

There is a great deal going on in these lines: not just that Sulpicia has experienced love and wants to tell about it, but the importance of "repute"—what people will say about her hiding or telling it, and how the "repute" will be more shameful to her if she hides it than if she tells it. The convoluted and rather unpoetic language slows us down, forcing us to think through and try to grasp the meaning behind it. For a similarly complex combination of thought and syntax, see the translation of Sulpicia 6, below.

Sulpicia's work is generally dated to the late 20s B.C.E.—that is, to the heyday of Roman elegy—and it certainly contains familiar elegiac elements, particularly the centrality of the lover's emotions, the celebration of a beloved under a pseudonym, the presentation of both happiness and betrayal. But the combination of her gender and her social class makes it impossible to place her comfortably in the elegiac cast of characters. Sulpicia calls herself *puella* in three of the epigrams (2.3, 3.1, 5.1), but her pedigree makes her far closer to Catullus's Lesbia (so often called *puella*) than to the working girls of elegy. Since she is the poet, it is better to think of her in the role of the elegiac lover, with Cerinthus cast as the pseudonymous *puella*. But Sulpicia has not simply given us an elegiac affair with the sexes reversed. Almost every line in the epigrams demonstrates the impossibility of such a simple substitution and reveals the great distance between the agency and choices of an aristocratic young woman like Sulpicia and her male counterparts. A female elegiac lover must do things differently.

The world sketched for us in the epigrams is one of both privilege and constraint, each dependent on the other. Sulpicia comes from a great family—a position that both fortifies and limits her. She shows the inbred haughtiness of the aristocrat in reminding the unfaithful Cerinthus just who she is (Sulpicia 4.3–4):

> The toga and a whore, weighted with wool's creel, may be your
> Greater concern than Servius's daughter, Sulpicia.

Her position notwithstanding, however, the self-determination so important to the male elegists is unavailable to Sulpicia. As we see in her second epigram, she cannot choose even where to spend her birthday; that is a decision for Messalla. When he accedes to her pleas in the end, she rejoices *to be permitted* to do what she wants (Sulpicia 3.2):

> I am allowed to spend my birthday now at Rome.

The self-determination of her male counterparts largely consists in their espousing elegiac morality—choosing private over public in life as in poetry. Sulpicia, a young woman sheltered and watched over in her uncle's care, can have nothing *but* a private life that she has no part in choosing. Nonetheless, we may still see her as following the elegists but invoking a different kind of self-determination, the only one open to her. If the active life was de rigueur for men of Sulpicia's class, modesty and care of reputation were the appropriate life for women. As we have seen, the male elegists reject or at least play with society's expectations, substituting their own choices, which are also choices about poetry. Sulpicia may be doing something similar in her own realm when she plays on the idea of reputation in her program poem. Let us look again at the opening couplet (Sulpicia 1.1–2):

> At last a love has come such that repute of having hid it
> Would shame me more than had I laid it bare.

Society would expect a young woman like Sulpicia either not to be spoken of at all or else to be spoken of but little and in the highest possible terms; but Sulpicia rejects that expectation. She wants the "repute" not only of having consummated her love but also of having bared the fact to the world. Like the elegists, she is expressing a choice that is about poetry as well as life; the "repute" that she has in mind is not only what will be said about her but also the fame that will be won by her poetry.

THE POEMS

Albii Tibulli

Liber Primus

I

Divitias alius fulvo sibi congerat auro
    Et teneat culti iugera multa soli,
Quem labor assiduus vicino terreat hoste,
    Martia cui somnos classica pulsa fugent:
Me mea paupertas vitam traducat inertem,   5
    Dum meus assiduo luceat igne focus.
Ipse seram teneras maturo tempore vites
    Rusticus et facili grandia poma manu:
Nec Spes destituat, sed frugum semper acervos
    Praebeat et pleno pinguia musta lacu.   10
Nam veneror, seu stipes habet desertus in agris
    Seu vetus in trivio florida serta lapis,
Et quodcunque mihi pomum novus educat annus,
    Libatum agricolae ponitur ante deo.
Flava Ceres, tibi sit nostro de rure corona   15
    Spicea quae templi pendeat ante fores:
Pomosisque ruber custos ponatur in hortis,
    Terreat ut saeva falce, Priapus, aves.
Vos quoque, felicis quondam, nunc pauperis agri
    Custodes, fertis munera vestra, Lares.   20
Tunc vitula innumeros lustrabat caesa iuvencos,
    Nunc agna exigui est hostia parva soli.

The text followed is that of *Albii Tibulli aliorumque Carmina,* ed. G. Luck
(Stuttgart, 1988). Major variations are listed below.

1.5: *me* for *mi.*
1.15: *sit* for *fit.*

Albius Tibullus

Book 1

1. Choosing a Life

Let another man pile for himself gleaming heaps of gold
   And claim for tillage many an acre of land,
Whom constant toil scares, with the enemy nearby,
   And Mars's trumpets blare his sleep to flight:
Let my poverty direct me through a lazy life   5
   As long as a steadfast flame gleams upon my hearth.
I will plant young vines, when the time is right, myself
   And well-grown trees, a farmer with practiced hand.
Let Spes, sure patron, supply me with heaps of grain,
   With a rich vintage from the brimming vat.   10
I worship, whether a lone stump stands garlanded in the fields
   Or an ancient stone where the ways cross.
And the very first fruit the new year rears for me
   Is placed as a gift before the farmer's god.
Blond Ceres, be yours the garland made from ears of corn   15
   From our farm, to hang before your temple doors.
In the fruited garden post you, Priapus, a ruddy guard
   To scare the birds with his savage pruning hook.
And you, guardian Lares, take your due from these fields,
   Fortunate in times past, now become so poor.   20
Then a calf's sacrifice purified our herd of bulls;
   Now a lamb is the slim gift for our scanty plot.

Agna cadet vobis, quam circum rustica pubes
  Clamet 'io messes et bona vina date'.
Iam mihi, iam possim contentus vivere parvo   25
  Nec semper longae deditus esse viae,
Sed Canis aestivos ortus vitare sub umbra
  Arboris ad rivos praetereuntis aquae.
Nec tamen interdum pudeat tenuisse bidentem
  Aut stimulo tardos increpuisse boves,   30
Non agnamve sinu pigeat fetumve capellae
  Desertum oblita matre referre domum.
At vos exiguo pecori, furesque lupique,
  Parcite: de magno est praeda petenda grege.
Hinc ego pastoremque meum lustrare quotannis   35
  Et placidam soleo spargere lacte Palem.
Adsitis, divi, neu vos e paupere mensa
  Dona nec e puris spernite fictilibus.
Fictilia antiquus primum sibi fecit agrestis
  Pocula, de facili composuitque luto.   40
Non ego divitias patrum fructusque requiro
  Quos tulit antiquo condita messis avo:
Parva seges satis est, satis requiescere lecto,
  Si licet, et solito membra levare toro.
Quam iuvat immites ventos audire cubantem   45
  Et dominam tenero continuisse sinu,
Aut, gelidas hibernus aquas cum fuderit Auster,
  Securum somnos igne iuvante sequi!
Hoc mihi contingat: sit dives iure, furorem
  Qui maris et tristes ferre potest pluvias.   50
O quantum est auri potius pereatque smaragdi
  Quam fleat ob nostras ulla puella vias.
Te bellare decet terra, Messalla, marique,
  Ut domus hostiles praeferat exuvias:
Me retinent vinctum formosae vincla puellae,   55
  Et sedeo duras ianitor ante fores.
Non ego laudari curo: mea Delia, tecum
  Dum modo sim, quaeso segnis inersque vocer.

1.43: The reminiscence of Catullus 31.10 confirms *lecto*.
1.48: *igne* for *imbre*.

The lamb will be yours. Round it let our country folk cry,
  Here comes the harvest! Make our wine good!
Now I myself, now I could be content to live this simple life,   25
  Not always committed to a far campaign,
To shun the sweltering rise of Canis beneath
  A tree's shade by a stream of gliding water.
Meanwhile it would not bring disgrace to hold a sheep,
  Or urge on the lagging oxen with my goad,   30
Nor shame to carry home a lamb in my embrace
  Or a lost kid, abandoned by its mother.
As for you, thieves and wolves, spare this meager flock.
  Go find your booty among a grander herd.
I like to purify my shepherd every year   35
  And sprinkle kindly Pales with some milk.
Gods, be with us here, and reject not gifts that come
  From a simple table or from pure earthenware.
Earthen cups the farmer of old first modeled
  And molded them for himself from pliant mud.   40
I do not need the wealth or the harvests of my forebears,
  The yield stocked away by our ancient founder.
A small plot is enough; enough to rest at home
  If I may refresh my limbs on a familiar bed.
How good when drowsing to hear the pitiless wind   45
  And to hold my lady in a light embrace,
Or when wintry Auster lets loose his frosty rains,
  Safe, to pursue dreams by a comforting fire!
This is what I want! With my blessing let the man be rich
  Who can stand grim rains and the roaring of the sea.   50
Yes, it is far better to let all gold and emeralds go
  Than that for my journeys any girl should weep.
Messalla, for you it is right to make war on land and sea
  So that your house display the enemy's spoils.
But the bonds of a beautiful girl bind me fast,   55
  And I sit, a watchman before unyielding doors.
I care nothing for fame: my Delia, as long as I am with you,
  Slacker I want them to call me, and a shirk.

Te spectem, suprema mihi cum venerit hora,
    Te teneam moriens deficiente manu.   60
Flebis et arsuro positum me, Delia, lecto,
    Tristibus et lacrimis oscula mixta dabis.
Flebis: non tua sunt duro praecordia ferro
    Vincta, neque in tenero stat tibi corde silex.
Illo non iuvenis poterit de funere quisquam   65
    Lumina, non virgo, sicca referre domum.
Tu Manes ne laede meos, sed parce solutis
    Crinibus et teneris, Delia, parce genis.
Interea, dum fata sinunt, iungamus amores:
    Iam veniet tenebris Mors adoperta caput,   70
Iam subrepet iners aetas, nec amare decebit,
    Dicere nec cano blanditias capite.
Nunc levis est tractanda Venus, dum frangere postes
    Non pudet et rixas inseruisse iuvat.
Hic ego dux milesque bonus: vos, signa tubaeque,   75
    Ite procul, cupidis vulnera ferte viris.
Ferte et opes: ego composito securus acervo
    Despiciam dites despiciamque famem.

2

Adde merum vinoque novos compesce dolores,
    Occupet ut fessi lumina victa sopor,
Neu quisquam multo percussum tempora Baccho
    Excitet, infelix dum requiescit amor.
Nam posita est nostrae custodia saeva puellae,   5
    Clauditur et dura ianua firma sera.
Ianua difficilis domini, te verberet imber,
    Te Iovis imperio fulmina missa petant.
Ianua, iam pateas uni mihi, victa querelis,
    Neu furtim verso cardine aperta sones.   10
Et mala siqua tibi dixit dementia nostra,
    Ignoscas: capiti sint precor illa meo.
Te meminisse decet, quae plurima voce peregi
    Supplice, cum posti florida serta darem.

2.7: *domini* for *dominae*.

I want to be looking at you when my final hour arrives,
    To hold you at the last with my failing hand.   60
You will weep for me, Delia, when I lie upon my kindling pyre;
    You will give me kisses mingled with sad tears.
You will weep. No iron hardness sheaths your breast
    In bonds. No flint lies in your tender heart.
No boy can carry home from that funeral,   65
    No girl either, eyes that are dry.
But be gentle with my Manes, Delia, and forbear
    To rip your hair or to tear your gentle cheeks.
Meantime, while the Fates allow, let us join in love.
    Soon Mors will come, her head veiled in shadow.   70
Soon slack age will slink in. We will suit no more for love,
    For uttering sweet nothings with our heads gone gray.
Now let fickle Venus be our sport while there's no shame
    In breaking down doors and it's fun to make a row.
Here is where I am a good soldier in chief! You, flags and trumpets,   75
    Go away! Bring wounds to greedy men!
And bring them money too. My modest heap secured,
    I will look down on wealth, look down on hunger too.

2. Locked Out

Pour the wine. Check fresh grief with drink,
    That sleep may seize my tired-out, vanquished eyes.
And leave this man in peace, his brain lashed with Bacchus's
    Plenty, while unfortunate love's at rest.
A cruel guard has been set over my girl.   5
    An immovable bolt keeps the door shut.
Door as hard as your master, may you be slashed by the rain.
    May lightning strike you, sped by Jove's command.
Door, yield to my groans, and open only for me,
    Soundlessly now upon your turning pin.   10
If my madness ever uttered curses against you,
    Forgive me. May they light on my own head!
Please remember all the things I said when I was pleading
    And placing flowered wreaths upon your doorpost.

Tu quoque ne timide custodes, Delia, falle,   15
    Audendum est: fortes adiuvat ipsa Venus.
Illa favet, seu quis iuvenis nova limina temptat,
    Seu reserat fixo dente puella fores:
Illa docet furtim molli derepere lecto,
    Illa pedem nullo ponere posse sono,   20
Illa viro coram nutus conferre loquaces
    Blandaque compositis abdere verba notis.
Nec docet hoc omnis, sed quos nec inertia tardat
    Nec vetat obscura surgere nocte timor.
En ego cum tenebris tota vagor anxius urbe,   25
    . . . .
Nec sinit occurrat quisquam, qui corpora ferro
    Vulneret aut rapta praemia veste petat.
Quisquis amore tenetur, eat tutusque sacerque
    Qualibet: insidias non timuisse decet.   30
Non mihi pigra nocent hibernae frigora noctis,
    Non mihi, cum multa decidit imber aqua.
Non labor hic laedit, reseret modo Delia postes
    Et vocet ad digiti me taciturna sonum.
Parcite luminibus, seu vir seu femina fias   35
    Obvia: celari vult sua furta Venus.
Neu strepitu terrete pedum, neu quaerite nomen,
    Neu prope fulgenti lumina ferte face.
Siquis et imprudens aspexerit, occulat ille
    Perque deos omnes se meminisse neget: 40
Nam fuerit quicumque loquax, is sanguine natam,
    Is Venerem e rabido sentiet esse mari.
Nec tamen huic credet coniunx tuus, ut mihi verax
    Pollicita est magico saga ministerio.
Hanc ego de caelo ducentem sidera vidi,   45
    Fluminis haec rapidi carmine vertit iter,
Haec cantu finditque solum Manesque sepulcris
    Elicit et tepido devocat ossa rogo.
Iam tenet infernas magico stridore catervas,
    Iam iubet aspersas lacte referre pedem: 50
Cum libet, haec tristi depellit nubila caelo,
    Cum libet, aestivo convocat orbe nives.
Sola tenere malas Medeae dicitur herbas,
    Sola feros Hecatae perdomuisse canes.

Delia, too, be not afraid to outwit the guards.   15
   Time for courage: Venus supports the brave!
She helps the boy who tries his luck at a new doorway,
   And the girl who opens up the bolted gate.
She teaches you to steal quietly out of your soft bed,
   To put your foot down with no sound at all,   20
To give speaking nods right before your husband
   And hide your *yes* in prearrangèd signs.
But she instructs not all, only those with enterprise
   Whom fear cannot stop from rising late at night.
Watch me, worried wanderer through the whole city's darkness!   25
. . . .
She lets no one threaten me or wield a wounding
   Knife, or make off with my cloak as prize.
Whoever is guided by love, let him have a safe and blessèd passage
   Wherever he wants. There are no tricks to fear.   30
No harm for me from numbing frosts of a winter's night,
   No harm from flooding rains falling in torrents.
This effort is no trouble, were Delia to unlatch the door,
   And give a quiet sign with her tapping finger.
Man or woman, should you draw near, do not look!   35
   Venus likes her intrigues kept well hid.
Do not startle with your footfall or ask names,
   Or bring nearby your torch's shining gleam.
Should someone foolish catch a glimpse, let him keep it secret
   And swear by all the gods he saw not a thing.   40
For the one who talks will soon find that Venus
   Was born from blood and from the raging sea.
In my case your husband will not believe a word,
   A trusty witch assured me with her magic.
I have seen her lead the stars down from the sky   45
   And turn with song a headlong river's course,
With chant split the earth, and draw Manes from tombs
   And summon down bones from the lukewarm pyre.
Now she rules the multitudes of hell with a sorcerer's shriek;
   Now spatters them with milk and sends them off.   50
She banishes, just as she pleases, clouds from the lowering heavens;
   When she pleases, she calls snow from summer skies.
She's the only one, they say, who can use Medea's poisons;
   She alone tames Hecate's terrible hounds.

Haec mihi composuit cantus, quis fallere posses: 55
　　Ter cane, ter dictis despue carminibus.
Ille nihil poterit de nobis credere cuiquam,
　　Non sibi, si in molli viderit ipse toro.
Tu tamen abstineas aliis: nam cetera cernet
　　Omnia: de me uno sentiet ipse nihil. 60
Quid? credam? nempe haec eadem se dixit amores
　　Cantibus aut herbis solvere posse meos,
Et me lustravit taedis, et nocte serena
　　Concidit ad magicos hostia pulla deos.
Non ego, totus abesset amor, sed mutuus esset, 65
　　Orabam, nec te posse carere velim.
Ferreus ille fuit, qui, te cum posset habere,
　　Maluerit praedas stultus et arma sequi.
Ille licet Cilicum victas agat ante catervas,
　　Ponat et in capto Martia castra solo, 70
Totus et argento contextus, totus et auro
　　Insideat celeri conspiciendus equo,
Ipse boves, mea sim tecum modo Delia, possim
　　Iungere et in solito pascere monte pecus:
Et te dum liceat teneris retinere lacertis, 75
　　Mollis et inculta sit mihi somnus humo.
Quid Tyrio recubare toro sine amore secundo
　　Prodest, cum fletu nox vigilanda venit?
Nam neque tum plumae nec stragula picta soporem
　　Nec sonitus placidae ducere possit aquae. 80
Num Veneris magnae violavi numina verbo
　　Et mea nunc poenas impia lingua luit?
Num feror incestus sedes adiisse deorum
　　Sertaque de sanctis deripuisse focis?
Non ego, si merui, dubitem procumbere templis 85
　　Et dare sacratis oscula liminibus,
Non ego tellurem genibus perrepere supplex
　　Et miserum sancto tundere poste caput.
At tu, qui laetus rides mala nostra, caveto
　　Mox tibi: non uni saeviet usque deus. 90

2.74: *in solito* for *in solo*.
2.81: *violavi* for *violavit*.

For me she made chants you can use to deceive.   55
    Sing them thrice, and spit thrice when you have sung.
Then he cannot believe anyone talking about us, not even
    If he himself has seen us on the soft bed.
But you had better forsake others. For everything else
    He will have eyes. He is only blind to me.   60
Can I believe it? This same creature with chants and herbs
    Has said she can release me from my love.
She encircled me with fire, and on a moonlit night
    A dusky victim fell to the magic gods.
I did not pray to be altogether freed from love.   65
    It should be shared. I would not live without you.
That was a man of iron who, though he could have you, chose
    In folly to chase war and the spoils of war.
He may drive crowds of conquered Cilicians before him,
    May pitch Mars's camp on ground that he has seized,   70
All armored with silver, all armored with gold—
    A cynosure mounted on a speedy steed.
If only I were with you, Delia, I could yoke our oxen
    And bring the flock to feed on its familiar hill.
As long as I might hold you in my tender arms   75
    Even on hard ground I would sleep softly.
What profit to lie loveless on a couch of Tyrian hue
    When the wakeful night approaches with its tears?
Neither a bed of feathers nor a painted coverlet
    Nor the sound of quiet water could bring sleep.   80
Have I, with one word, blasphemed Venus's godhead?
    Does my guilty tongue now pay what it deserves?
Did I, impious, approach the seats of the gods
    Or snatch one garland from their holy fire?
If guilty, I would collapse prostrate before their temples   85
    And bestow a kiss upon their holy thresholds.
A suppliant, I would not hesitate to crawl the earth on my knees
    And pound my poor head against their sacred door.
But you, all laughter at my plight, watch out. Your time awaits.
    The god will not always rage against me alone.   90

Vidi ego, qui iuvenum miseros lusisset amores,
    Post Veneris vinclis subdere colla senem,
Et sibi blanditias tremula componere voce
    Et manibus canas fingere velle comas:
Stare nec ante fores puduit caraeve puellae   95
    Ancillam medio detinuisse foro.
Hunc puer, hunc iuvenis turba circumterit arta,
    Despuit in molles et sibi quisque sinus.
At mihi parce, Venus: semper tibi dedita servit
    Mens mea: quid messes uris acerba tuas?   100

3

Ibitis Aegaeas sine me, Messalla, per undas,
    O utinam memores ipse cohorsque mei!
Me tenet ignotis aegrum Phaeacia terris:
    Abstineas avidas, Mors, modo nigra, manus.
Abstineas, Mors atra, precor: non hic mihi mater   5
    Quae legat in maestos ossa perusta sinus,
Non soror, Assyrios cineri quae dedat odores,
    Et fleat effusis ante sepulcra comis,
Delia non usquam; quae me quam mitteret urbe,
    Dicitur ante omnes consuluisse deos.   10
Illa sacras pueri sortes ter sustulit: illi
    Rettulit e trinis omina certa puer.
Cuncta dabant reditus: tamen est deterrita nunquam,
    Quin fleret nostras respiceretque vias.
Ipse ego solator, cum iam mandata dedissem,   15
    Quaerebam tardas anxius usque moras.
Aut ego sum causatus aves aut omina dira,
    Saturni aut sacrum me tenuisse diem.
O quotiens ingressus iter mihi tristia dixi
    Offensum in porta signa dedisse pedem!   20
Audeat invito ne quis discedere Amore,
    Aut sciat egressum se prohibente deo.

3.4: *modo nigra* for *precor atra.*
3.11: *pueri* for *puero.*
3.14: *respiceretque* for *respueretque.*
3.22: *sciat* for *sciet.*

I saw one who mocked the passions of young men
    Later in age bow his neck to Venus's chains,
And utter blandishments with a shaky voice, and
    With fingers yearn to comb his graying hair.
He was not ashamed to stand before his sweetheart's doorway   95
    Or entreat her servant right in the Forum.
Then boys, then young men crowd tightly all about him,
    And each one spits in his own soft clothes for luck.
But spare me, Venus. My mind is your devoted liege,
    Forever. Why do you bitterly burn your fields?   100

3. Ill on Phaeacia, Thinking of Delia

You will cross the Aegean waves without me, Messalla. I hope
    You and our company will keep mindful of me,
Sick, in the clasp of Phaeacia's unknown land, I pray:
    Black Mors, unclasp your grasping hands.
Unclasp, dark Mors, I pray. There is no mother here   5
    To gather my charred bones to her grieving lap,
No sister to offer my ashes Assyrian incense,
    To let her hair down and weep beside the tomb.
Above all no Delia. Before she sent me from the city,
    She consulted every single god, they say.   10
Thrice she drew the boy's sacred lots. Thrice
    From the crossroads the boy's omens brought her good luck.
They all promised return, yet she did not refrain
    From looking back, and weeping at my journey.
Last orders given, I soothed her, and in my unease   15
    I sought and sought good reasons for delay.
Birds were my excuse, or every dread omen,
    Or Saturn's holy day, to hold me back.
How many times, already started out, did I say
    That my foot tripped at the gate, a bad-luck sign!   20
Let no one dare depart if Amor thinks otherwise,
    Or he will know he went with the god opposed.

Quid tua nunc Isis mihi, Delia, quid mihi prosunt
    Illa tua totiens aera repulsa manu,
Quidve, pie dum sacra colis, pureque lavari
    Te (memini) et puro secubuisse toro?   25
Nunc, dea, nunc succurre mihi (nam posse mederi
    Picta docet templis multa tabella tuis),
Ut mea votivas persolvens Delia voces
    Ante sacras lino tecta fores sedeat   30
Bisque die resoluta comas tibi dicere laudes
    Insignis turba debeat in Pharia.
At mihi contingat patrios celebrare Penates
    Reddereque antiquo menstrua tura Lari.
Quam bene Saturno vivebant rege prius quam   35
    Tellus in longas est patefacta vias!
Nondum caeruleas pinus contempserat undas
    Effusum ventis praebueratque sinum,
Nec vagus ignotis repetens compendia terris
    Presserat externa navita merce ratem.   · 40
Illo non validus subiit iuga tempore taurus,
    Non domito frenos ore momordit equus,
Non domus ulla fores habuit, non fixus in agris,
    Qui regeret certis finibus arva, lapis.
Ipsae mella dabant quercus, ultroque ferebant   45
    Obvia securis ubera lactis oves.
Non acies, non ira fuit, non bella, nec ensem
    Immiti saevus duxerat arte faber.
Nunc Iove sub domino caedes et vulnera semper,
    Nunc mare, nunc leti multa reperta via est.   50
Parce, pater: timidum non me periuria terrent,
    Non dicta in sanctos impia verba deos.
Quod si fatales iam nunc explevimus annos,
    Fac lapis inscriptis stet super ossa notis:
'Hic iacet immiti consumptus morte Tibullus,   55
    Messallam terra dum sequiturque mari.'
Sed me, quod facilis tenero sum semper Amori,
    Ipsa Venus campos ducet in Elysios.

3.25: *lavari* for *lavaris*.
3.29: *voces* for *noctes*.

What good to me now your Isis, Delia? What help for me
    Those bronze rattles you have so often clanged?
What about those rites, purification by water,   25
    That chaste bed where you slept alone, I recall?
Come now, Goddess, help me now. The many paintings
    In your temples teach us your healing power,
So that my Delia may fulfill her prayerful vows,
    Sit clothed in linen before your sacred doors,   30
And twice a day, her hair down, sing your due praises,
    Standing out among the Pharian crowd.
But to me may it fall to praise my own Penates,
    With incense honor the ancient Lar each month.
How well they lived while King Saturn ruled,   35
    Before the world was open to long treks,
Back before a ship of pine had scorned the slate-dark waves
    And offered to the winds its billowing sails,
Before the rover, seeking profit in unknown lands,
    Had weighted down his boat with foreign wares!   40
Back then the powerful bull had not submitted to the yoke
    Nor did the horse champ its bit with obedient mouth.
Houses had no doors, and nowhere in the fields
    Did stone mark plowlands with assurèd bounds.
The very oaks gave honey, and gladly sheep   45
    Brought milk-filled udders home to the carefree.
No troops then, no rage, no wars, no savage smithy
    Hammered out swords with merciless artistry.
But now, Jove's subjects, we ever have slaughter and wounds,
    Now the sea, now many a route to death.   50
Leave off, Father. No false vows have scared me into fear,
    No impieties voiced against the holy gods.
If my time has come, and I have filled my fated years,
    Place these words carved above my bones:
Here lies Tibullus, destroyed by savage Mors,   55
    Following Messalla over land and sea.
Because I am ever yielding toward tender Amor, Venus
    Herself will lead me to the Elysian Fields.

Hic choreae cantusque vigent, passimque vagantes
   Dulce sonant tenui gutture carmen aves,   60
Fert casiam non culta seges, totosque per agros
   Floret odoratis terra benigna rosis:
Hic iuvenum series teneris immixta puellis
   Ludit, et assidue proelia miscet Amor.
Illic est, cuicumque rapax mors venit amanti,   65
   Et gerit insigni myrtea serta coma.
At scelerata iacet sedes in nocte profunda
   Abdita, quam circum flumina nigra sonant:
Tisiphoneque impexa feros pro crinibus angues
   Saevit, et huc illuc impia turba fugit: 70
Tum niger in porta serpentum Cerberus ore
   Stridet et aeratas excubat ante fores.
Illic Iunonem tentare Ixionis ausi
   Versantur celeri noxia membra rota,
Porrectusque novem Tityos per iugera terrae   75
   Assiduas atro viscere pascit aves.
Tantalus est illic, et circum stagna: sed acrem
   Iam iam poturi deserit unda sitim,
Et Danai proles, Veneris quod numina laesit,
   In cava Lethaeas dolia portat aquas.   80
Illic sit, quicumque meos violavit amores,
   Optavit lentas et mihi militias.
At tu casta precor maneas, sanctique pudoris
   Assideat custos sedula semper anus.
Haec tibi fabellas referat positaque lucerna   85
   Deducat plena stamina longa colu,
At circa gravibus pensis affixa puella
   Paulatim somno fessa remittat opus.
Tum veniam subito, nec quisquam nuntiet ante,
   Sed videar caelo missus adesse tibi.   90
Tunc mihi, qualis eris, longos turbata capillos,
   Obvia nudato, Delia, curre pede.
Hoc precor, hunc illum nobis Aurora nitentem
   Luciferum roseis candida portet equis.

3.69: *impexa* for *implexa.*
3.71: *in porta* for *intorto.*

Here thrive dance and song, while everywhere
    Roaming birds sing sweet from delicate throats. 60
Cinnamon grows untended, and over all the fields
    Kind earth blooms with richly pungent rose.
Here a team of boys plays among tender girls
    While Amor ceaselessly stirs up strife.
He is here, whichever lover encountered plundering Mors, 65
    And wears myrtle garlands on his glimmering hair.
But there is a place for sinners, hidden in deepest night,
    Ringed about with the roar of rivers black.
Tisiphone rages, a tangle of horrible snaky tresses,
    And now here, now there, the wicked crowd takes flight. 70
Then at the gate dark serpent-tongued Cerberus
    Howls and keeps watch before the brazen doors.
Here are the vile limbs, whirled on a rapid wheel,
    Of Ixion, who dared assault Juno,
And Tityos, stretched out over nine acres of ground, 75
    With his dark vitals gluts ever-feeding birds.
Tantalus stands poised among quiet waters
    That again and again elude his bitter thirst.
And Danaus's daughters, sacrilegious to Venus, lug
    Lethaean water into their punctured vats. 80
This is the place for whoever has defiled my true love
    And wished on me long, drawn-out war.
But, I beseech you, keep chaste, and may your attentive nurse
    Stay by you always to guard your modesty.
Let her tell you stories, and when the lamp is lit, 85
    Let her guide down long strands from full distaff,
While bit by bit the servant girl, intent upon her weighty work,
    Grows drowsy, then slips slowly off to sleep.
Then may I suddenly arrive, with no warning ahead.
    May my presence seem to you sent from heaven above. 90
And, just as you are, Delia, long hair all tangled
    And feet bare, hurry and run to me.
May Aurora then bring us this Lucifer—this I pray—
    Brilliant with roseate steeds, on that bright day.

4

'Sic umbrosa tibi contingant tecta, Priape,
    Ne capiti soles, ne noceantque nives:
Quae tua formosos cepit sollertia? certe
    Non tibi barba nitet, non tibi culta coma est,
Nudus et hibernae producis frigora brumae,   5
    Nudus et aestivi tempora sicca Canis.'
Sic ego: tum Bacchi respondit rustica proles
    Armatus curva sic mihi falce deus:
'O fuge te tenerae puerorum credere turbae:
    Nam causam iusti semper amoris habent.   10
Hic placet, angustis quod equum compescit habenis:
    Hic placidam niveo pectore pellit aquam:
Hic, quia fortis adest audacia, cepit: at illi
    Virgineus teneras stat pudor ante genas.
Sed ne te capiant, primo si forte negabit,   15
    Taedia: paulatim sub iuga colla dabit.
Longa dies homini docuit parere leones,
    Longa dies molli saxa peredit aqua:
Annus in apricis maturat collibus uvas,
    Annus agit certa lucida signa vice.   20
Nec iurare time: Veneris periuria venti
    Irrita per terras et freta summa ferunt.
Gratia magna Iovi: vetuit pater ipse valere,
    Iurasset cupide quicquid ineptus amor:
Perque suas impune sinit Dictynna sagittas   25
    Affirmes crines perque Minerva suos.
At si tardus eris, errabis: transilit aetas
    Quam cito! non segnis stat remeatque dies.
Quam cito purpureos deperdit terra colores,
    Quam cito formosas populus alta comas!   30
Quam iacet, infirmae venere ubi fata senectae,
    Qui prior Eleo est carcere missus equus!

4.15: *negabit* for *negarit.*
4.27: *tardus eris* for *tardueris.*
4.30: *alta* for *alba.*

4. Priapus's Advice

"May shady arbors ever be your lot, Priapus;
  May neither suns nor snows damage your head:
Teach me the tricks you employ to entice pretty youths.
  Your beard is ugly; your hair, a mess.
Naked you live through the frosts of winter's cold;   5
  Naked, Canis's season of summer drought."
That is what I said. Bacchus's rustic son, a god,
  With his weapon the curved pruning hook, then replied:
"Do not, I urge you, trust in the delicate troupe of boys.
  They always present a good reason for their love.   10
You like this one for the way he reins in a horse;
  This one breasts the waves with snowy chest.
This one seized his prey with brazen manners; a virgin's chastity
  Stands guard before that one's delicate cheeks.
Let not frustration seize you if at first he chance to refuse.   15
  Bit by bit he will bend his neck to the yoke.
Time's passage taught lions obedience to man.
  Time's passage has gnawed through rocks with a soft stream.
The year brings grapes their ripeness on the sunny hills.
  The year in sure cycle herds its gleaming stars.   20
Be not afraid of swearing oaths; Venus's lies are borne by the wind
  Harmlessly over the land and the seas' high crest.
Great thanks to Father Jove: he decreed that lovers' oaths
  Sworn in passion's folly count for naught.
Dictynna lets you swear unpunished by her arrows;   25
  By Minerva's tresses you may make a pledge.
Any delay will be your mistake. How swiftly age travels on!
  Eager day neither pauses nor returns.
How swiftly the land loses its colored flowers!
  How swiftly the tall poplar loses its lovely leaves!   30
How lifeless the worn-out steed, when the Fates of age have come,
  That once sprang from the starting gate at Elis!

Vidi iam iuvenem, premeret cum serior aetas,
    Maerentem stultos praeteriisse dies.
Crudeles divi! serpens novus exuit annos: 35
    Formae non ullam fata dedere moram.
Solis aeterna est Baccho Phoeboque iuventa:
    Nam decet intonsus crinis utrumque deum.
Tu, puero quodcumque tuo temptare libebit,
    Cedas: obsequio plurima vincet amor.   40
Neu comes ire neges, quamvis via longa paretur
    Et Canis arenti torreat arva siti,
Quamvis praetexens picta ferrugine caelum
    Venturam admittat nubifer Eurus aquam:
Vel si caeruleas puppi volet ire per undas,   45
    Ipse levem remo per freta pelle ratem.
Nec te paeniteat duros subiisse labores
    Aut operae insuetas atteruisse manus,
Nec, velit insidiis altas si claudere valles,
    Dum placeas, umeri retia ferre negent: 50
Si volet arma, levi tentabis ludere dextra;
    Saepe dabis nudum, vincat ut ille, latus.
Tum tibi mitis erit, rapias tum cara licebit
    Oscula: pugnabit, sed tamen apta dabit.
Rapta dabit primo, post adferet ipse roganti,   55
    Post etiam collo se implicuisse volet.
Heu male nunc artes miseras haec saecula tractant:
    Iam tener assuevit munera velle puer.
At tu, qui Venerem docuisti vendere primus,
    Quisquis es, infelix urgeat ossa lapis.   60
Pieridas, pueri, doctos et amate poetas,
    Aurea nec superent munera Pieridas.
Carmine purpurea est Nisi coma: carmina ni sint,
    Ex humero Pelopis non nituisset ebur.
Quem referunt Musae, vivet, dum robora tellus,   65
    Dum caelum stellas, dum vehet amnis aquas.

4.33: *iuvenem* for *iuveni*.
4.34: *stultos* for *stulte*.
4.43: *picta* for *picea*.
4.54: *tamen apta* for *male rapta*.
4.55: *adferet* for *auferet*.

I once saw a youth, as old age pressed him down,
  Lament that stupid time had passed him by.
Cruel gods! In spring the snake shrugs off its years:
  The Fates have granted beauty no reprieve.   35
Only Phoebus and Bacchus have eternal youth:
  Hair uncut is becoming to both gods.
Whatever it is your boy decides to try, give in.
  A yielding love will usually have its way.
Go along if he wants you to, even if he's taking a long trip,   40
  And Canis burns the fields with parching thirst,
Although cloud-filled Eurus, fringing the sky with purple tint,
  Darkly announces rain is close at hand.
Or if he wants to roam the blue-gray sea by yacht,
  Yourself push the lithe skiff oared through the waves.   45
Shy not away from enduring hard toils,
  Or from wearing away your hands unused to work.
If he wants to go trapping far in the deepest valleys,
  Provided you please, let your shoulders bear the nets.   50
He wants to fence: try to spar with easy thrust. Often
  You will bare your unarmed side so he can win.
Then he will be gentle, and you will chance to snatch dear kisses.
  He will object, yet he will grant what suits.
First he will give them snatched, soon offer them asked,   55
  Then eagerly wrap himself about your neck.
Alas, our times now deal in hurtful arts.
  Now a tender youth is used to seeking gifts.
You who first taught Venus was a vendor's prize,
  Whoever you are, may a wretched rock press your bones.   60
Boys, you must love the Pierides and their learnèd poets.
  Golden gifts should not best the Pierides.
It was song that brought purple to Nisus's hair. Without song
  From Pelops's shoulder ivory would not shine.
He whom the Muses support will live as long as the earth
    bears trees,
  The sky has stars, and streams carry water's flow.   65

At qui non audit Musas, qui vendit amorem,
　　Idaeae currus ille sequatur Opis
Et tercentenas erroribus expleat urbes
　　Et secet ad Phrygios vilia membra modos.　　　　　　70
Blanditiis vult esse locum Venus: illa querelis
　　Supplicibus, miseris fletibus illa favet.'
Haec mihi, quae canerem Titio, deus edidit ore:
　　Sed Titium coniunx haec meminisse vetat.
Pareat ille suae: vos me celebrate magistrum,　　　　　　75
　　Quos male habet multa callidus arte puer.
Gloria cuique sua est: me, qui spernuntur, amantes
　　Consultent: cunctis ianua nostra patet.
Tempus erit, cum me Veneris praecepta ferentem
　　Deducat iuvenum sedula turba senem.　　　　　　80
Heu heu, quam Marathus lento me torquet amore!
　　Deficiunt artes deficiuntque doli.
Parce, puer, quaeso, ne turpis fabula fiam,
　　Cum mea ridebunt vana magisteria.

5

Asper eram et bene discidium me ferre loquebar:
　　At mihi nunc longe gloria fortis abest.
Namque agor ut per plana citus sola verbere turben
　　Quem celer assueta versat ab arte puer.
Ure ferum et torque, libeat ne dicere quicquam　　　　　5
　　Magnificum posthac: horrida verba doma.
Parce tamen, per te furtivi foedera lecti,
　　Per Venerem quaeso compositumque caput.
Ille ego, cum tristi morbo defessa iaceres,
　　Te dicor votis eripuisse meis,　　　　　　10
Ipseque te circumlustravi sulphure puro,
　　Carmine cum magico praecinuisset anus:
Ipse procuravi, ne possent saeva nocere
　　Somnia, ter salsa deveneranda mola:

4.81: *torquet* for *torret*.
5.11: *te* for *ter*.
5.13: *saeva* for *scaeva*.
5.14: *somnia* for *omina*.

Who ignores the Muses and traffics in purchased love,
    Let him follow the chariot of Ida's Ops,
Girdle three hundred cities in restless wandering,
    And sever his worthless members to the beat of Phrygian strains.   70
Venus likes us to flatter. She also sides with suppliants
    Weeping and with abject cries for help."
Thus the god addressed me. I wanted to tell this to Titius,
    But this Titius's wife would not let him remember.
Let him obey her. Yet honor me as master, you   75
    Whom a clever boy controls through art's many tricks!
Everyone is famous for something. Let spurned lovers
    Find counsel with me: the door is open to all.
One day an eager crowd of youths will escort me,
    Expounding in old age Venus's rules.   80
Alas! Alas, how Marathus twists me in love's supple toils!
    My arts have failed, and all my tricks have failed.
Spare me, I ask, dear boy, or I will become an ugly tale,
    When they laugh at the fraud as my teachings fail.

5. The Wealthy Lover

I was angry, and bragged I could handle separation,
    But now my bold swagger is long gone away.
I am driven like a top, whirled around a level field,
    That a swift boy has lashed with his usual skill.
Scorch and rack my wildness lest hereafter I find joy   5
    In boastfulness: tame my threatening words.
Only please be kind! I plead by the stealthy concord of our bed,
    By Venus and your head posed next to mine.
I am he, when you lay exhausted from dread disease,
    Who is said by my vows to have rescued you from danger,   10
I who circled around you with the purest sulfur
    While an old crone intoned her magic song.
I devoted myself, lest savage dreams torment you,
    To have them thrice exorcised with salted grain.

Ipse ego velatus lino tunicisque solutis   15
    Vota novem Triviae nocte silente dedi.
Omnia persolvi: fruitur nunc alter amore,
    Et precibus felix utitur ille meis.
At mihi felicem vitam, si salva fuisses,
    Fingebam demens, sed renuente deo.   20
'Rura colam, frugumque aderit mea Delia custos,
    Area dum messes sole calente teret,
Aut mihi servabit plenis in lintribus uvas
    Pressaque veloci candida musta pede.
Consuescet numerare pecus, consuescet amantis   25
    Garrulus in dominae ludere verna sinu.
Illa deo sciet agricolae pro vitibus uvam,
    Pro segete spicas, pro grege ferre dapem.
Illa regat cunctos, illi sint omnia curae:
    At iuvet in tota me nihil esse domo.   30
Huc veniet Messalla meus, cui dulcia poma
    Delia selectis detrahat arboribus,
Et, tantum venerata virum, cui sedula curet,
    Cui paret atque epulas ipsa ministra gerat.'
Haec mihi fingebam quae nunc Eurusque Notusque   35
    Iactat odoratos vota per Armenios.
Saepe ego temptavi curas depellere vino,
    At dolor in lacrimas verterat omne merum.
Saepe aliam tenui, sed iam cum gaudia adirem,
    Admonuit dominae deseruitque Venus.   40
Tunc me discedens devotum femina dixit,
    Ah pudet, et narrat scire nefanda meam.
Non facit hoc verbis, facie tenerisque lacertis
    Devovet et flavis nostra puella comis.
Talis ad Haemonium Nereis Pelea quondam   45
    Vecta est frenato caerula pisce Thetis.
Haec nocuere mihi quod adest huic dives amator:
    Venit in exitium callida lena meum.
Sanguineas edat illa dapes atque ore cruento
    Tristia cum multo pocula felle bibat: 50

5.43: *verbis* for *herbis*.
5.47: *haec* for *at*.

Veiled in linen and with my shirt undone   15
    I offered nine prayers to Trivia in the still of night.
I fulfilled all. Now another enjoys my love,
    Blessed to obtain the benefit of my prayers.
Foolish, I imagined what a blessèd life I would have
    If you found a cure. The god said *No!*   20
"I will live in the country, my Delia with me to watch over the crops,
    When the floor will thresh the grain during summer's warmth.
Or she will set aside grapes in overflowing vats,
    Or gleaming must, crushed by a rushing foot.
She will get used to counting cattle; a chattering slave child will get
        used to   25
    Playing in his loving mistress's lap.
To the farmer god she will learn to bring grapes on behalf of
        the vines,
    Ears of corn for the harvest, a feast for the flock.
Let her take care of it all, preside over everyone:
    My pleasure to be as nothing in the whole house.   30
Here my Messalla will come. For him Delia
    Will pick sweet apples from the choicest trees.
Worshipful and eager to give service to such a man
    She will prepare the banquet and be the serving maid."
I was imagining these prayers that now Eurus and Notus   35
    Drive across Armenia's scented race.
Often have I tried to banish my woes with wine,
    But grief has transformed my drink all to tears.
Often have I held another; but then, when I came near to joy,
    Venus warned me of my mistress, then disappeared.   40
And the woman, taking her leave, called me bewitched.
    She says—the shame!—that my girl knows things not to be told!
Not with spells does she this. Our girl bewitches
    With her face, her kindly arms, and her golden hair.
Such was the blue-eyed Nereid Thetis, riding long ago   45
    To Haemonian Peleus on her bridled fish.
This has brought me harm: her rich lover is at home
    And the crafty bawd has occasioned my ruin.
Let her food be bloody, and let her gore-streaked mouth
    Gulp down glum goblets slathered with gall,   50

Hanc volitent animae circum sua fata querentes
    Semper et e tectis strix violenta canat:
Ipsa fame stimulante furens herbasque sepulcris
    Quaerat et a saevis ossa relicta lupis,
Currat et inguinibus nudis ululetque per urbem,   55
    Post agat e triviis aspera turba canum.
Eveniet: dat signa deus: sunt numina amanti,
    Saevit et iniusta lege relicta Venus.
At tu quam primum sagae praecepta rapacis
    Desere: non donis vincitur omnis amor.   60
Pauper erit praesto semper tibi, pauper adibit
    Primus et in tenero fixus erit latere,
Pauper in angusto fidus comes agmine turbae
    Subicietque manus efficietque viam,
Pauper ad occultos furtim deducet amicos   65
    Vinclaque de niveo detrahet ipse pede.
Heu canimus frustra, nec verbis fatiscit
    Ianua, sed plena est percutienda manu.
At tu, qui potior nunc es, mea fata caveto:
    Versatur celeri Fors levis orbe rotae.   70
Non frustra quidam iam nunc in limine perstat
    Sedulus ac crebro prospicit ac refugit,
Et simulat transire domum, mox deinde recurrit,
    Solus et ante ipsas excreat usque fores.
Nescio quid furtivus amor parat: utere quaeso,   75
    Dum licet: in liquida nat tibi linter aqua.

6

Semper, ut inducar, blandos offers mihi vultus,
    Post tamen es misero tristis et asper, Amor.
Quid tibi, saeve, rei mecum est? an gloria magna est
    Insidias homini composuisse deum?
Iam mihi tenduntur casses: iam Delia furtim   5
    Nescio quem tacita callida nocte fovet.

5.64: *subicietque* for *subiicietque*.
5.69: *fata* for *furta*.

And may ghosts bewailing their doom ever swarm round her head
    And screech owl hoot threats from the roofs.
And, mad from hunger's goad, may she seek grass in graveyards,
    Seek bones left behind by wild wolves.
Let her run, sex bared. Let her howl through the town, then   55
    Angry dog pack drive her from where roads meet.
It will happen. God sends signs; a lover has his deities.
    Venus rages when left for an unjust bond.
But you with all speed leave behind the greedy witch's rules:
    Not every love is overcome by gifts.   60
A poor man will always be ready for you; a poor man will be
    First to hand and affixed to your tender side.
A poor man, trusty shepherd through the crowd's narrow throng,
    Will thrust forth his hand and make you a path.
A poor man will lead you cunningly to sly friends, himself   65
    Remove the thongs from your snowy foot.
Alas, our song is vain. The door does not gape open from
      words' force
    But must be beaten by generous hands.
But you, who now feel so sure, be wary of my lot.
    Fickle Fors turns on a nimble wheel.   70
Someone even now, and not in vain, stands in the doorway,
    Eagerly looks here and there, makes to withdraw.
He pretends to be going home. Then before you know it
    There he is at the very door, alone, clearing his throat.
Secret love ever plots. Be advised: take pleasure while you may.   75
    Your skiff is swimming over calm water's sway.

6. Delia's Husband and Mother

Always to draw me on you grant me kindly looks.
    Later, Amor, to the forlorn you are dour and hostile.
Fierce creature, why bother with me? Is it such a noble thing
    For a god to contrive snares for a mere man?
For the nets are stretched for me; now wily Delia secretly   5
    Warms a stranger in the quiet of the night.

Illa quidem iurata negat, sed credere durum est:
  Sic etiam de me pernegat usque viro.
Ipse miser docui quo posset ludere pacto
  Custodes: heu heu, nunc premor arte mea,   10
Fingere tunc didicit causas, ut sola cubaret,
  Cardine tunc tacito vertere posse fores,
Tunc sucos herbasque dedi, quis livor abiret,
  Quem facit impresso mutua dente Venus.
At tu, fallacis coniunx incaute puellae,   15
  Me quoque servato, peccet ut illa nihil,
Neu iuvenes celebret multo sermone, caveto,
  Neve cubet laxo pectus aperta sinu,
Neu te decipiat nutu, digitoque liquorem
  Ne trahat et mensae ducat in orbe notas.   20
Exibit cum saepe, time, seu visere dicet
  Sacra Bonae maribus non adeunda Deae.
At, mihi si credas, illam sequar unus ad aras:
  Tunc mihi non oculis sit timuisse meis.
Saepe, velut gemmas eius signumque probarem,   25
  Per causam memini me tetigisse manum:
Saepe mero somnum peperi tibi, at ipse bibebam
  Sobria supposita pocula victor aqua.
Non ego te laesi prudens (ignosce fatenti):
  Iussit Amor: contra quis ferat arma deos?   30
Ille ego sum, nec me iam dicere vera pudebit,
  Latrabat tota cui tua nocte canis.
Quid tenera tibi coniuge opus? tua si bona nescis
  Servare, heu, frustra clavis inest foribus.
Te tenet, absentes alios suspirat amores   35
  Et simulat subito condoluisse caput.
At mihi servandam credas: non saeva recuso
  Verbera, detrecto non ego vincla pedum.
Tum procul absitis, quisquis colit arte capillos,
  Et fluit effuso cui toga laxa sinu: 40
Quisquis et occurret, ne possit crimen habere,
  Stet procul aut alia †stet procul† ante via.
Sic fieri iubet ipse deus, sic magna sacerdos
  Est mihi divino vaticinata sono.

She offers her denial under oath, but it is hard to trust.
    Ever she denies me to her husband, in the same way.
Unlucky me! I taught her how to baffle her guards,
    Alas! Alas, I am deceived now by my own tricks! 10
She learned then to construct reasons why she should sleep alone,
    Then how to open a door on silent hinge.
Then I gave her juices and herbs to eradicate the bruises
    Our tooth marks dug from Venus's own give and take.
But you, heedless husband of a deceiving girl, 15
    Watch out for me, too, lest she stray.
Watch out lest she frequent the youths in conversation
    Or lie at rest, robe loose, bosom revealed,
Or trick you with a secret nod, or with her finger
    Write on the round table in a spill of wine. 20
Watch out when she will often wander off or announce a visit
    To the rites of Bona Dea—no men allowed.
Trust me: alone I will follow her right to the altar.
    I need not worry then about my sight.
Often, I recall, with good reason I touched her hand, 25
    As if to judge her jewels or her ring.
Often I got you sleepy with wine while I myself, in charge,
    Drank sober goblets with water in its stead.
Now I never meant to offend you. (A confession should bring
        pardon.)
    Amor gave the orders. Who will take arms against the gods? 30
After all, I am the one—I'll not be ashamed to admit it now—
    At whom your dog kept barking all night long.
Why do you need a tender bride? If you cannot guard your goods,
    Alas, the key rests vainly in the door.
She holds you; she sighs for other lovers elsewhere. 35
    Suddenly she pretends a frightful headache.
Leave her to me to guard! I can take savage
    Whippings. I do not refuse shackles on my feet.
But keep your distance, you with your elegant coiffeurs
    And togas loose with slackened folds. 40
And whoever meets us, lest guilt be his, let him
    Stand afar—on another road, stand afar.
The god himself arranges this; this his high priestess
    Has foretold to me in very sacred tones.

Haec ubi Bellonae motu est agitata, nec acrem   45
    Flammam, non amens verbera torta timet:
Ipsa bipenne suos caedit violenta lacertos
    Sanguineque effuso spargit inulta deam,
Statque latus praefixa veru, stat saucia pectus,
    Et canit eventus, quos dea magna monet: 50
'Parcite, quam custodit Amor, violare puellam,
    Ne pigeat magno post didicisse malo.
Attigeris, labentur opes, ut vulnere nostro
    Sanguis, ut hic ventis diripiturque cinis.'
Et tibi nescio quas dixit, mea Delia, poenas   55
    Si tamen admittas, sit precor illa levis.
Non ego te propter parco tibi, sed tua mater
    Me movet atque iras aurea vincit anus.
Haec mihi te adducit tenebris multoque timore
    Coniungit nostras clam taciturna manus,   60
Haec foribusque manet noctu me affixa proculque
    Cognoscit strepitus me veniente pedum.
Vive diu mihi, dulcis anus: proprios ego tecum,
    Sit modo fas, annos contribuisse velim.
Te semper natamque tuam te propter amabo: 65
    Quicquid agit, sanguis est tamen illa tuos.
Sit modo casta, doce, quamvis non vitta ligatos
    Impediat crines nec stola longa pedes.
Et mihi sint durae leges, laudare nec ullam
    Possim ego, quin oculos appetat illa meos,   70
Et siquid peccasse putet, ducarque capillis
    In medias pronus proripiarque vias.
Non ego te pulsare velim, sed, venerit iste
    Si furor, optarim non habuisse manus.
Nec saevo sis casta metu, sed mente fideli   75
    Mutuus absenti te mihi servet amor.
At, quae fida fuit nulli, post victa senecta
    Ducit inops tremula stamina torta manu
Firmaque conductis adnectit licia telis
    Tractaque de niveo vellere ducta putat.   80
Hanc animo gaudente vident iuvenumque catervae
    Conmemorant merito tot mala ferre senem,

And she, stirred by Bellona's prompt, in wildness   45
    Fears not flame's bite or twistings of the lash.
Unhurt she fiercely strikes her own arms with an ax
    And spatters the goddess with a flow of blood.
She stands, side pierced by a spear, stands with wounded breast,
    Singing out the warnings the great goddess gives: 50
Refrain from hurting the girl whom Amor takes under his care
    Lest from great hurt you later learn regret.
Touch her once; wealth will drift away as blood flows
    From our wound, as this ash is swept up by the winds.
My Delia, as for the penalties she pronounced: 55
    If you grant someone entrance, I pray she may be gentle.
It is not on your account that I refrain. Your ancient mother's
    Golden self touches me and soothes my wrath.
She leads you to me in the shadows and joins our two hands
    In silent secrecy, quite terrified.   60
By night she waits for me, rooted outside in the doorway,
    Knows the sound of my step as I approach from afar.
Live long, my sweet crone! I would like, were I able, to share
    With you a few of my allotted years.
I will always love you, and on your account I will love your daughter.   65
    Whatever she does, her blood remains still yours.
Urge her to be faithful though no ribbons bind her hair,
    Though her feet aren't covered beneath a matron's robes.
Even if the rules be hard, lest Delia gouge my eyes
    I would have no will to praise another girl.   70
If she thinks I've strayed, may I be hauled off by the hair
    And, face down, be dragged through the center of the streets.
I would never wish to strike you. If such a rage should descend
    On me I would sooner have my hands cut off.
Be pure not from savage fright but from a faithful heart.   75
    May our mutual love keep you safe when I am away.
But the woman who is true to none, broken then by age and want,
    Spins out the twisted thread with trembling hands,
For hire makes fast the leashes to the loom
    And scrubs down the skeins, pulled from their snowy fleece.   80
And the gangs of boys will watch her with gleeful heart and agree:
    Evil upon evil the hag deserves to bear.

Hanc Venus ex alto flentem sublimis Olympo
  Spectat et infidis quam sit acerba monet.
Haec aliis maledicta cadant: nos, Delia, amoris   85
  Exemplum cana simus uterque coma.

7

Hunc cecinere diem Parcae fatalia nentes
  Stamina, non ulli dissoluenda deo;
Hunc fore, Aquitanas posset qui fundere gentes,
  Quem tremeret forti milite victus Atax.
Evenere: novos pubes Romana triumphos   5
  Vidit et evinctos bracchia capta duces;
At te victrices lauros, Messalla, gerentem
  Portabat niveis currus eburnus equis.
Non sine me est tibi partus honos: Tarbella Pyrene
  Testis et Oceani litora Santonici,   10
Testis Arar Rhodanusque celer magnusque Garunna,
  Carnuti et flavi caerula lympha Liger.
An te, Cydne, canam, tacitis qui leniter undis
  Caeruleus placidis per vada serpis aquis,
Quantus et aetherio contingens vertice nubes   15
  Frigidus intonsos Taurus alat Cilicas?
Quid? referam, ut volitet crebras intacta per urbes
  Alba Palaestino sancta columba Syro,
Utque maris vastum prospectet turribus aequor
  Prima ratem ventis credere docta Tyros,   20
Qualis et, arentes cum findit Sirius agros,
  Fertilis aestiva Nilus abundet aqua?
Nile pater, quanam possum te dicere causa
  Aut quibus in terris occuluisse caput?
Te propter nullos tellus tua postulat imbres,   25
  Arida nec Pluvio supplicat herba Iovi.
Te canit utque suum pubes miratur Osirim
  Barbara, Memphiten plangere docta bovem.

7.8: *portabat* for *portabit*.
7.11: *Arar Rhodanusque* for *Atur Duranusque*.
7.13: *tacitis* for *tractis*.

Aloft on high Olympus, Venus observes her in tears
    And warns the fickle just how pitiless she is prone.
Let these curses fall elsewhere, Delia. Let us each be   85
    A model of love as our hair grows white to see.

7. Messalla's Birthday

The Parcae sang this day, weaving their fateful threads,
    To be annulled by no god's power:
That he would be born who could subdue the Aquitanian race,
    And, conquered by his brave troops, the Atax would cower.
And it all came to pass. The youth of Rome saw fresh triumphs,   5
    Captured chiefs, hands bound behind their backs.
But you, Messalla, wreathed with the victor's laurels,
    Snow-bright horses carried on an ivory car.
Not without me was your glory gained: Tarbellian Pyrene
    Bore witness, and the shores of the Santonic Ocean.   10
The Arar bears witness, swift Rhodanus, mighty Garunna,
    The blond Carnuti, and the Liger's blue flow.
Or, Cydnus, shall I sing of you, who softly in your silent path
    Wind your blue course with gentle wave,
Or how the grand Taurus, touching the clouds with its soaring crest, 15
    In chill nourishes the unshorn Cilices?
Further, shall I add how the holy white dove from Syrian Palaestine
    Flies unharmed among the crowded cities,
And Tyros that first learned to entrust a vessel to the winds
    Observes from its towers vast reaches of the sea?   20
And in what mass, when Sirius splits the burning fields,
    The Nilus overbounds with summer's fertile flow?
Father Nilus, for what reason and in what region
    Can I declare you have hidden away your head?
Because of you your land need not ask for rain,   25
    The dry grass offers no prayer to Jupiter Pluvius.
Foreign youths sing of you and worship you as their Osiris,
    Schooled to lament Memphis's sacred bull.

Primus aratra manu sollerti fecit Osiris
    Et teneram ferro sollicitavit humum,   30
Primus inexpertae commisit semina terrae
    Pomaque non notis legit ab arboribus.
Hic docuit teneram palis adiungere vitem,
    Hic viridem dura caedere falce comam:
Illi iucundos primum matura sapores   35
    Expressa incultis uva dedit pedibus.
Ille liquor docuit voces inflectere cantu,
    Movit et ad certos nescia membra modos,
Bacchus et agricolae magno confecta labore
    Pectora tristitiae dissoluenda dedit.   40
Bacchus et afflictis requiem mortalibus affert,
    Crura licet dura compede pulsa sonent.
Non tibi sunt tristes curae nec luctus, Osiri,
    Sed chorus et cantus et levis aptus amor,
Sed varii flores et frons redimita corymbis,   45
    Fusa sed ad teneros lutea palla pedes
Et Tyriae vestes et dulcis tibia cantu
    Et levis occultis conscia cista sacris.
Huc ades et Genium ludis Geniumque choreis
    Concelebra et multo tempora funde mero: 50
Illius et nitido stillent unguenta capillo,
    Et capite et collo mollia serta gerat.
Sic venias hodierne: tibi dem turis honores,
    Liba et Mopsopio dulcia melle feram.
At tibi succrescat proles, quae facta parentis   55
    Augeat et circa stet venerata senem.
Nec taceat monumenta viae, quem Tuscula tellus
    Candidaque antiquo detinet Alba Lare.
Namque opibus congesta tuis hic glarea dura
    Sternitur, hic apta iungitur arte silex.   60
Te canet agricola, a magna cum venerit urbe
    Serus inoffensum rettuleritque pedem.
At tu, Natalis multos celebrande per annos,
    Candidior semper candidiorque veni.

7.40: *tristitiae* for *laetitiae*.
7.49: *ludis* for *ludo*.

Osiris was the first to make a plow with skillful hand,
  And with iron stirred the delicate earth.   30
The first who entrusted seed to the untried ground
  And gathered fruit from trees as yet unnamed.
He taught how to fasten the tender vines to stakes,
  He, to prune the green shoots with a hard blade.
The ripened grapes, trod by unlearnèd feet,   35
  For him first yielded him their sweet savors.
That liquid taught men how to mold the voice in song
  And moved their ignorant limbs to assurèd beats.
Bacchus provided a way to release sadness
  From the hearts of farmers, done in by heavy labor.   40
Bacchus brings peace to men in torment, even when
  The clangor of hard chains beats against their legs.
Sadness and heartbreak and mourning are not for you, Osiris,
  But nimble love is fitting, and dance, and song,
But an abundance of flowers, a brow wreathed in clustered berries,   45
  But a yellow gown flowing down to delicate feet,
And Tyrian robes, and the flute's sweet song,
  And the light basket, witness to secret rites.
Come here: with games celebrate your Genius, with dances
  Your Genius, and drench his head with a flood of wine.   50
Let unguents drip from his shining tresses;
  Let him show off soft wreaths on his brow and neck.
Come then today: I would grant you the grace of incense
  And carry cakes perfumed with the honey of Mopsus.
May your offspring flourish, to enhance their father's deeds,   55
  And, revered themselves, gather round the old man.
Nor should he, whom Tusculum and bright Alba keep from his
      ancestral Lar,
  Fail to praise the memorial that is your road.
For here, built by your resource, the hard gravel is laid level,
  And here rock slabs are conjoined with fitting art.   60
Then the farmer on his late return from the great city will sing
  Your praises, when his foot need never stumble.
And you, Natalis, to be sung throughout many a year,
  Ever brighter, brighter still, make your way here.

8

Non ego celari possum, quid nutus amantis
    Quidve ferant miti lenia verba sono.
Nec mihi sunt sortes nec conscia fibra deorum,
    Praecinit eventus nec mihi cantus avis:
Ipsa Venus magico religatum bracchia nodo   5
    Perdocuit multis non sine verberibus.
Desine dissimulare: deus crudelius urit,
    Quos videt invitos succubuisse sibi.
Quid tibi nunc molles prodest coluisse capillos
    Saepe et mutatas disposuisse comas,   10
Quid fuco splendente genas ornasse, quid ungues
    Artificis docta subsecuisse manu?
Frustra iam vestes, frustra mutantur amictus,
    Ansaque compressos colligat arta pedes.
Illa placet, quamvis inculto venerit ore   15
    Nec nitidum tarda compserit arte caput.
Num te carminibus, num te pallentibus herbis
    Devovit tacitae tempore noctis anus?
Cantus vicinis fruges traducit ab agris,
    Cantus et iratae detinet anguis iter,   20
Cantus et e curru Lunam deducere tentat
    Et faceret, si non aera recurva sonent.
Quid queror, heu, misero carmen nocuisse, quid herbas?
    Forma nihil magicis utitur auxiliis:
Sed corpus tetigisse nocet, sed longa dedisse   25
    Oscula, sed femini conseruisse femur.
Nec tu difficilis puero tamen esse memento
    (Persequitur poenis tristia facta Venus),
Munera nec poscas: det munera canus amator,
    Ut foveat molli frigida membra sinu.   30
Carior est auro iuvenis, cui levia fulgent
    Ora nec amplexus aspera barba terit.
Huic tu candentes humero suppone lacertos,
    Et regum magnae despiciantur opes.

8.30: *foveat* for *foveas*.

8. Marathus and Pholoe

What mean the nods of a lover cannot escape me
    Or what the soothing words with their gentle hum.
I use no lots or entrails privy to the gods,
    Nor does birdsong chant for me the time to come.
Venus herself has fully instructed me with lash after lash,   5
    My arms bound tightly with a magic knot.
Stop this pretending! The god burns more cruelly
    Those whom he sees yielding unwillingly to him.
What good does it do you now to adorn your soft tresses,
    So often to arrange and dye your hair?   10
What good to have smoothed your cheeks with brilliant rouge,
    what good
    To have trimmed your nails with an artiste's practiced hand?
Vain now are your clothes varied, vain your robes,
    And a tight shoe cramps your tightened feet.
She makes a hit though she arrives with her face not made up.   15
    She has not taken time to design her bright hair.
Has some crone bewitched you in the dead of night,
    Bewitched with charm songs, bewitched with pale-green herbs?
Song draws crops away from a neighbor's field;
    Song holds back the course of an angered snake.   20
Song attempts to drag Luna from her car,
    And would do so, did curved brasses not resound.
Poor, poor me! Why do I complain about the harm of song, the harm
    of herbs?
    Beauty resorts not at all to magic aids.
But harm comes from touching her body, from bestowing lingering   25
    Kisses, from entangling leg with leg.
And you remember, try not to be too rigid with the boy.
    (Venus craves recompense for misdeeds.)
Ask not for gifts. Let the white-haired lover bestow gifts,
    Payment to warm his chill limbs in a soft lap.   30
A youth, whose smooth cheeks glow, is worth more than gold,
    And no rough beard grates against your embrace.
Beneath his shoulders wrap your gleaming arms.
    Heap scorn on the wealth that kings amass!

At Venus inveniet puero concumbere furtim,   35
    Dum timet, et teneros conserere usque sinus,
Et dare anhelanti pugnantibus umida linguis
    Oscula et in collo figere dente notas.
Non lapis hanc gemmaeque iuvent, quae frigore sola
    Dormiat et nulli sit cupienda viro.   40
Heu sero revocatur amor seroque iuventa,
    Cum vetus infecit cana senecta caput.
Tum studium formae est: coma tunc mutatur, ut annos
    Dissimulet viridi cortice tincta nucis.
Tollere tunc cura est albos a stirpe capillos   45
    Et faciem dempta pelle referre novam.
At tu, dum primi floret tibi temporis aetas,
    Utere: non tardo labitur illa pede.
Neu Marathum torque: puero quae gloria victo est?
    In veteres esto dura, puella, senes.   50
Parce precor tenero: non illi sontica causa est,
    Sed nimius luto corpora tingit amor.
Vel miser absenti maestas quam saepe querelas
    Coniicit, et lacrimis omnia plena madent!
'Quid me spernis?' ait. 'poterat custodia vinci: 55
    Ipse dedit cupidis fallere posse deus.
Nota Venus furtiva mihi est, ut lenis agatur
    Spiritus, ut nec dent oscula rapta sonum:
Et possum media quamvis obrepere nocte
    Et strepitu nullo clam reserare fores.   60
Quid prosunt artes, miserum si spernit amantem
    Et fugit ex ipso saeva puella toro
Vel cum promittit, subito sed perfida fallit,
    Et mihi nox multis est vigilanda malis?
Dum mihi venturam fingo, quodcumque movetur,   65
    Illius credo tunc sonuisse pedes.'
Desistas lacrimare, puer: non frangitur illa,
    Et tua iam fletu lumina fessa tument.
Oderunt, Pholoe, moneo, fastidia divi,
    Nec prodest sanctis tura dedisse focis.   70

8.36: *timet* for *tumet*.

Venus will find a sly way for you to lie with the fearful lad   35
    And even to mesh chest with tender chest,
And, as your tongues do battle, while he pants to bestow wet
    Kisses, to pierce tooth marks in his neck.
Jeweled stones are no good to a girl sleeping alone,
    Cold, for no man an object of desire.   40
Alas, you cry for love too late, for youth too late,
    When white-haired age has streaked your ancient head.
And then you work at beauty. Your hair changes color,
    Dyed with a fresh nut's bark to disguise your years.
The task then is to pull every white hair out by the roots,   45
    To bring a new glow back to ravished cheeks.
But while your life's bloom is at its springtime, put it to use.
    It glides away from you on fleeting foot.
Stop torturing Marathus! What glory in conquering a youth?
    Save your hardness, girl, for old codgers.   50
Please be good to the tender lad. What he has is not catching.
    A surfeit of love dyes our bodies yellow.
Poor thing, how often he has hurled sad complaints at you,
    Away, and everything gets filled with tears.
"Why do you scorn me?" he says. "The guard could have been
        overcome.   55
    The god himself grants lovers the power to dupe.
I know Venus and her thefts: the drawing of gentle breath,
    Kisses snatched without making even a sound.
At will I can sneak in during the middle of the night
    And unlatch the door in secret without a squeak.   60
But what good are these skills if such a horrid girl
    Scorns her poor lover and flees right out of bed,
Or she can promise to come but suddenly betray her trust,
    And I must endure the night with its many woes?
I imagine she is on her way, and whatever it is that stirs,   65
    I believe then I hear approaching her own footfall."
Stop this weeping, my boy. It will never break her,
    And your exhausted eyes are now swollen with tears.
And, Pholoe, I warn you, the gods loathe pride. It does no good
    To have heaped up incense at their holy shrines.   70

Hic Marathus quondam miseros ludebat amantes,
    Nescius ultorem post caput esse deum:
Saepe etiam lacrimas fertur risisse dolentis
    Et cupidum ficta detinuisse mora:
Nunc omnes odit fastus, nunc displicet illi   75
    Quaecumque opposita est ianua dura sera.
At te poena manet, ni desinis esse superba.
    Quam cupies votis hunc revocare diem!

9

Quid mihi, si fueras miseros laesurus amores,
    Foedera per divos, clam violanda, dabas?
A miser, et siquis primo periuria celat,
    Sera tamen tacitis Poena venit pedibus.
Parcite, caelestes: aequum est impune licere   5
    Numina formosis laedere vestra semel.
Lucra petens habili tauros adiungit aratro
    Et durum terrae rusticus urget opus,
Lucra petituras freta per parentia ventis
    Ducunt instabiles sidera certa rates: 10
Muneribus meus est captus puer: at deus illa
    In cinerem et liquidas munera vertat aquas.
Iam mihi persolvet poenas, pulvisque decorem
    Detrahet et ventis horrida facta coma,
Uretur facies, urentur sole capilli,   15
    Deteret invalidos et via longa pedes.
Admonui quotiens 'auro ne pollue formam:
    Saepe solent auro multa subesse mala.
Divitiis captus siquis violavit amorem,
    Asperaque est illi difficilisque Venus.   20
Ure meum potius flamma caput et pete ferro
    Corpus et intorto verbere terga seca.
Nec tibi celandi spes sit peccare paranti:
    Scit deus, occultos qui vetat esse dolos.

9.1: *laesurus* for *lusurus.*
9.3: *a miser, et siquis* for *Ah! misere etsi quis.*

This Marathus once kept mocking wretched lovers, unaware
    That a vengeful god was right behind his back.
People say he often laughed at another's tears
    And thwarted the eager with feigned delay.
Now he can brook no hauteur; now he becomes upset
    When a hard door blocks the way with bolted lock.   75
If you do not desist from pride, then you can only pay.
    How you will pray to have back this lost day!

9. Marathus and an Old Man

If you were going to wrong my poor desires, why—by the gods!—
    Were you swearing your trust to sneak and betray me?
Poor, poor creature! Though someone at first conceal his lies,
    Yet Poena finally comes with silent step.
Gently, please, Gods! For the handsome it is right to injure   5
    Your powers without redress—but only once.
Seeking wealth the farmer fits his bulls to the nimble plow,
    Forcing a hard living from the land.
Seeking wealth through seas obedient to the winds
    Unsteady craft are led by the unerring stars.   10
My boy has been captured by gifts, but may the god
    Convert the gifts into ash and running water.
Then he will pay me the price. Dust will destroy
    His looks, and wind will roughen his hair.
His face will be burned, his locks burned from the sun,   15
    Travel afar will wear down his feeble feet.
How many times have I warned him: "Do not foul your beauty
        with gold!
    In gold many evils are likely to lurk.
And if, a prey to wealth, someone has violated love,
    Venus remains toward him both harsh and stern.   20
Rather burn my head with fire, attack my body
    With the sword, and slash my back with knotted whip.
Harbor no hope of hiding your readiness to sin. The god knows.
    His law allows no treachery to be masked.

Ipse deus tacito permisit lingua ministro
Ederet ut multo libera verba mero:
Ipse deus somno domitos emittere vocem
   Iussit et invitos facta tegenda loqui.'
Haec ego dicebam: nunc me flevisse loquentem,
   Nunc pudet ad teneros procubuisse pedes.
Tunc mihi iurabas nullo te divitis auri
   Pondere, non gemmis vendere velle fidem,
Non tibi si pretium Campania terra daretur,
   Non tibi si Bacchi cura Falernus ager.
Illis eriperes verbis mihi sidera caeli
   Lucere et pronas fulminis esse vias.
Quin etiam flebas: at non ego fallere doctus
   Tergebam humentes credulus usque genas.
Quid faceres, nisi et ipse fores in amore puellae?
   Sic precor exemplo sit levis illa tuo.
O quotiens, vobis ne quisquam conscius esset,
   Ipse comes multa lumina nocte tuli!
Saepe insperanti venit tibi munere nostro
   Et latuit clausas post adoperta fores.
Tum miser interii, stulte confisus amari:
   Nam poteram ad laqueos cautior esse tuos.
Quin etiam attonita laudes tibi mente canebam,
   At me nunc nostri Pieridumque pudet.
Illa velim rapida Vulcanus carmina flamma
   Torreat et liquida deleat amnis aqua.
Tu procul hinc absis, cui formam vendere cura est
   Et pretium plena grande referre manu.
At te, qui puerum donis corrumpere es ausus,
   Rideat assiduis uxor inulta dolis,
Et cum furtivo iuvenem lassaverit usu,
   Tecum interposita languida veste cubet.
Semper sint externa tuo vestigia lecto,
   Et pateat cupidis semper aperta domus:

25

30

35

40

45

50

55

9.35: *caeli* for *caelo.*

70

The god himself allowed the silent servant's tongue   25
    To utter open words when wine abounds.
The god himself has ordered those deep in sleep to give voice
    And, despite themselves, tell of deeds best left concealed."
Those were my words. Now I am ashamed of my tearful speech,
    Ashamed that I fell prostrate at delicate feet.   30
You promised me then that you would not wish to barter your
        trust
    For any weight of gold's riches or for gems,
Not if Campania's fields were yours for the payment,
    Not if Bacchus's favorite, the Falernian plain.
With those words you would make me mistrust heaven's
        shimmering   35
    Stars, the downward flow of rivers' paths.
You even started to weep; but I, ignorant of deceit,
    Naively blotted up your tear-drenched cheeks.
Why behave that way unless you have fallen for a girl?
    My prayer: May she be just as fickle as you have proved!   40
How many times, so no one would notice, I, your friend,
    Myself carried bright lights in dead of night!
Often, as my gift, she came to you when hope was lost,
    And lurked all hidden behind the closèd doors.
Then I died a sad death, foolishly sure I was loved,   45
    For I could have been more wary of your wiles!
Yes, with a crazed heart I even used to sing your praises.
    But now I feel shame for myself and the Pierides.
I would wish that Vulcan consume those poems with his speedy
        flame,
    And a stream wash them away with its clear flow.   50
And you, get far from my sight, bent on selling your beauty
    And reaping a huge reward with hand filled full.
But you who dared debase this boy with gifts, without reprisal
    May your wife scoff at you with deceit upon deceit.
And when she has worn out her young lover in secret mating,   55
    May she lie with you sated, sheets now between.
May there ever be traces of others on your bed
    And your house to the wanton ever lie wide open.

Nec lasciva soror dicatur plura bibisse
    Pocula vel plures emeruisse viros.   60
Illam saepe ferunt convivia ducere Baccho,
    Dum rota Luciferi provocet orta diem:
Illa nulla queat melius consumere noctem
    Aut operis varias disposuisse vices.
At tua perdidicit: nec tu, stultissime, sentis,   65
    Cum tibi non solita corpus ab arte movet.
Tune putas illam pro te componere corpus
    Aut tenues denso pectere dente comas?
Istane persuadet facies, auroque lacertos
    Vinciat et Tyrio prodeat apta sinu?   70
Non tibi, sed iuveni cuidam vult bella videri,
    Devoveat pro quo remque domumque tuam.
Nec facit hoc vitio, sed corpora foeda podagra
    Et senis amplexus culta puella fugit.
Huic tamen accubuit noster puer: hunc ego credam   75
    Cum trucibus Venerem iungere posse feris.
Blanditiasne meas aliis tu vendere es ausus,
    Tune aliis demens oscula ferre mea?
Tum flebis, cum me vinctum puer alter habebit
    Et geret in regno sceptra superba tuo.   80
At tua tum me poena iuvet, Venerique merenti
    Fixa notet casus aurea palma meos:
'Hanc tibi fallaci resolutus amore Tibullus
    Dedicat et grata sis, dea, mente rogat.'

10

Quis fuit, horrendos primus qui protulit enses?
    Quam ferus et vere ferreus ille fuit!
Tum caedes hominum generi, tum proelia nata,
    Tum brevior dirae mortis aperta via est.

9.61: *ferunt* for *ferant.*
9.72: *remque* for *teque.*

And may your lusty sister not be thought to outdo her
    In drinking or to have serviced more men.   60
For Bacchus they say she often prolongs her banquets
    Until Lucifer's rising wheels draw forth the day.
No better could she spend the night
    Or devise more varied ways to do her work.
But your wife has studied well. And you, fool of fools, do you
        not notice   65
    When she moves her body in a brand new way for you?
Do you think you are the one for whom she does her grooming
    Or dressed her thin tresses with the comb's thick tooth?
Is your face so alluring that she binds her arms with gold
    And ventures forth, dressed up in Tyrian garb?   70
You are not the boy she intends to show how pretty she is,
    You, whose money and whose house she is ruining with a curse.
And it is not her fault. A girl with any refinement flees
    An old man's kiss, the smell of festering gout.
Yet this is the one with whom my boy has lain. I might believe   75
    He is able to pair Venus with fierce beasts.
And you dared to sell my compliments elsewhere, fool,
    To hand over my kisses to other men?
Well will you weep when another youth holds me enslaved,
    And plants his haughty scepter in your realm.   80
Then may your punishment delight me, and a golden palm affixed
    To my saving Venus may mark my fate:
Tibullus, released from a false love, offers this, Goddess, to you.
    He asks that your kindly thoughts toward him be true.

10. To Valgius: Peace

Whoever was it who first discovered terrible swords?
    How feral and, yes, ferrous he really was!
Then slaughter came to mankind; then battles were born;
    Then a shorter path was opened to awful death.

An nihil ille miser meruit, nos ad mala nostra 5
    Vertimus, in saevas quod dedit ille feras?
Divitis hoc vitium est auri, nec bella fuerunt,
    Faginus astabat cum scyphus ante dapes.
Non arces, non vallus erat, somnumque petebat
    Securus varias dux gregis inter oves. 10
Tunc mihi vita foret, Valgi, nec tristia nossem
    Arma nec audissem corde micante tubam:
Nunc ad bella trahor, et iam quis forsitan hostis
    Haesura in nostro tela gerit latere.
Sed patrii servate Lares: aluistis et idem, 15
    Cursarem vestros cum tener ante pedes.
Neu pudeat prisco vos esse e stipite factos:
    Sic veteris sedes incoluistis avi.
Tunc melius tenuere fidem, cum paupere cultu
    Stabat in exigua ligneus aede deus. 20
Hic placatus erat, seu quis libaverat uvam,
    Seu dederat sanctae spicea serta comae:
Atque aliquis voti compos liba ipse ferebat
    Postque comes purum filia parva favum.
At nobis aerata, Lares, depellite tela, 25
    . . . . 25a
. . . . 25b
    Hostiaque e plena rustica porcus hara.
Hanc pura cum veste sequar myrtoque canistra
    Vincta geram, myrto vinctus et ipse caput.
Sic placeam vobis: alius sit fortis in armis
    Sternat et adversos Marte favente duces, 30
Ut mihi potanti possit sua dicere facta
    Miles et in mensa pingere castra mero.
Quis furor est atram bellis accersere mortem?
    Imminet et tacito clam venit illa pede.
Non seges est infra, non vinea culta, sed audax 35
    Cerberus et Stygiae navita turpis aquae:
Illic pertusisque genis ustoque capillo
    Errat ad obscuros pallida turba lacus.

But has the poor creature deserved the blame? It is we who turn   5
   To evil use what he offered us against savage beasts.
This is the cancer of gold's wealth. There were no wars
   When beechwood cups adorned our festive boards.
There were no forts, no palisades. The shepherd slept
   At ease among his flock's speckled sheep.   10
Oh, for life then, Valgius! I would have known no sadness of war
   Nor listened for the clarion with a quivering heart.
And now I am drawn into battle, and already perhaps some foe
   Brandishes a spear primed to pierce my flank.
But watch over me, ancestral Lares. You also cherished me   15
   When as a child I scampered before your feet.
Do not be ashamed to be crafted from an ancient trunk.
   As such you cherished our ancient forebear's home.
They held to their trust better then, when a wooden god,
   Dressed simply, stood in a slender shrine.   20
He was pleased if anyone had offered a grape
   Or given wreaths of grain for his holy head.
And, prayer answered, one brought offerings and, right behind,
   His small daughter with a fresh honeycomb.
But, Lares, ward off from us the weapons of bronze.   25
   . . . .   25a
. . . .   25b
   And a pig as country sacrifice from full pen.
I will follow the gift in a pristine robe, and I will bring baskets
      with myrtle
   Bound. My own head, too, is bound with myrtle.
Thus I might please you. Let another be brave at arms
   And lay low the enemy's chiefs with the blessing of Mars   30
So that as I drink he can boast of his deeds as soldier
   And in wine on the table sketch the camp for me.
What is this madness, summoning black Mors to war?
   She looms and secretly reaches us on silent tread.
No crops, no vineyards are worked down below, but there is
      Cerberus   35
   Bold, and the ugly sailor of the Stygian deep.
There with hollowed cheeks and burned-out hair
   An ashen host roams along the dull-lit pools.

Quam potius laudandus hic est, quem prole parata
    Occupat in parva pigra senecta casa.   40
Ipse suas sectatur oves, at filius agnos,
    Et calidam fesso comparat uxor aquam.
Sic ego sim, liceatque caput candescere canis,
    Temporis et prisci facta referre senem.
Interea Pax arva colat. Pax candida primum   45
    Duxit araturos sub iuga curva boves,
Pax aluit vites et sucos condidit uvae,
    Funderet ut nato testa paterna merum:
Pace bidens vomerque nitent, at tristia duri
    Militis in tenebris occupat arma situs,   50
Rusticus e lucoque vehit, male sobrius ipse,
    Uxorem plaustro progeniemque domum.
Sed Veneris tunc bella calent, scissosque capillos
    Femina perfractas conqueriturque fores:
Flet teneras obtusa genas, sed victor et ipse   55
    Flet sibi dementes tam valuisse manus.
At lascivus Amor rixae mala verba ministrat,
    Inter et iratum lentus utrumque sedet.
Ah lapis est ferrumque, suam quicumque puellam
    Verberat: e caelo deripit ille deos.   60
Sit satis e membris tenuem rescindere vestem,
    Sit satis ornatus dissolvisse comae,
Sit lacrimas movisse satis: quater ille beatus
    Quo tenera irato flere puella potest.
Sed manibus qui saevus erit, scutumque sudemque   65
    Is gerat et miti sit procul a Venere.
At nobis, Pax alma, veni spicamque teneto,
    Profluat et pomis candidus ante sinus.

10.39: *hic est* for *et hic.*
10.51: *lucoque vehit* for *luco revehit.*

How much more worthy of praise is he whom slow old age
    Grips, with children at hand, his dwelling small.   40
He accompanies his sheep; his son watches the lambs;
    His wife fetches warm water to ease fatigue.
Such may I be in old age—a lustrous, white-haired head
    With the chance to reminisce about times past.
Meanwhile let Pax care for the fields. Shining Pax first led   45
    Oxen under the curved yoke to the plow's work.
Pax nourished vines and established juice within the grape
    That a father's jug might pour wine for his son.
In time of Pax the hoe and share gleam; in the dark
    Rust seizes the tough soldier's gloomy arms.   50
And the peasant, himself scarcely sober, in his wagon
    Drives wife and children home from the sacred grove.
Then Venus's wars grow warm. A woman groans loudly.
    Her hair has been torn; her door is all broken in.
She weeps at the battering of her tender cheeks, yet the conqueror   55
    Himself weeps, too, for the strength of his maddened hands.
But lusty Amor purveys harsh words for the brawl,
    And sits in calm between the angry pair.
Oh, he is stone and iron, whoever strikes his girl!
    Such a one snatches the gods down from the sky.   60
Be it enough to have ripped her thin clothes from her body,
    Enough to have torn the ribbons from her hair,
Enough to have moved her to tears. Four times blessèd is he
    For whom a tender girl can weep at his wrath!
But whoever fights with his fists, let him carry both shield   65
    And pike, and keep his distance from gentle Venus.
But, kindly Pax, come here to us. Grasp the corn stalk.
    May your bright bosom brim with fruit, where'er you walk.

Liber Secundus

I

Quisquis adest, faveas: fruges lustramus et agros,
    Ritus ut a prisco traditus extat avo.
Bacche, veni, dulcisque tuis e cornibus uva
    Pendeat, et spicis tempora cinge, Ceres.
Luce sacra requiescat humus, requiescat arator,   5
    Et grave suspenso vomere cesset opus.
Solvite vincla iugis: nunc ad praesepia debent
    Plena coronato stare boves capite.
Omnia sint operata deo: non audeat ulla
    Lanificam pensis imposuisse manum.   10
Vos quoque abesse procul iubeo, discedat ab aris,
    Cui tulit hesterna gaudia nocte Venus.
Casta placent superis: pura cum veste venite
    Et manibus puris sumite fontis aquam.
Cernite, fulgentes ut eat sacer agnus ad aras   15
    Vinctaque post olea candida turba comas.
Di patrii, purgamus agros, purgamus agrestes:
    Vos mala de nostris pellite limitibus,
Neu seges eludat messem fallacibus herbis,
    Neu timeat celeres tardior agna lupos.   20
Tum nitidus plenis confisus rusticus agris
    Ingeret ardenti grandia ligna foco,
Turbaque vernarum, saturi bona signa coloni,
    Ludet et ex virgis extruet ante casas.
Eventura precor: viden ut felicibus extis   25
    Significet placidos nuntia fibra deos?
Nunc mihi fumosos veteris proferte Falernos
    Consulis et Chio solvite vincla cado.
Vina diem celebrent: non festa luce madere
    Est rubor, errantes et male ferre pedes.   30

1.17: *di* for *dii*.
1.21: *agris* for *areis*.

Book 2

1. Purifying the Fields

Whoever attends, be gracious: we purify crops and fields
    Just as the rite is passed to us from our ancient fathers.
Bacchus, come—may the sweet grape drape from your horns—
    And garland your brow with stalks of grain, Ceres.
May the earth rest in the sacred light; may the plowman rest.   5
    Let hard work stop, with plowshare hung up high.
Release the bonds from the yokes. It is the oxen's due
    To feed at full mangers with wreathèd heads.
Let all be done for the god's honor. Let no woman dare
    To place a working hand on the weights of wool.   10
I order you also to be off: let him depart far from these altars
    If last night Venus brought him pleasure.
Chastity pleases the gods. Come with spotless clothes.
    Take water from the fountain with spotless hands.
Look how the sacred lamb goes to the shining altar   15
    And the gleaming crowd follows, hair circled with olive.
Gods of our fathers, we cleanse the fields; we cleanse the farmers.
    Please drive ills away from off our bounds.
Let not the crop cheat the harvest through lying weeds.
    Nor let a slow-moving lamb dread the speedy wolves.   20
Now the beaming countryman, trusting in his full fields,
    Will heap great logs upon a roaring fire.
The home-bred crew of slaves, good sign of a wealthy farmer,
    Will sport and arrange houses made of twigs.
I pray for the outcome. Do you see how from fortunate entrails   25
    The foretelling innards give signs of favorable gods?
Bring forth now the ancient consul's smoky Falernian
    And remove for me the plugs from the Chian jug.
Let wines bring joy to the day. There is no shame to steep oneself
    On a festal day or go reeling on unsteady feet.   30

Sed 'bene Messallam' sua quisque ad pocula dicat,
    Nomen et absentis singula verba sonent.
Gentis Aquitanae celeber Messalla triumphis
    Et magna intonsis gloria victor avis,
Huc ades aspiraque mihi, dum carmine nostro   35
    Redditur agricolis gratia caelitibus.
Rura cano rurisque deos. his vita magistris
    Desuevit querna pellere glande famem:
Illi compositis primum docuere tigillis
    Exiguam viridi fronde operire domum,   40
Illi etiam tauros primi docuisse feruntur
    Servitium et plaustro supposuisse rotam.
Tunc victus abiere feri, tunc insita pomus,
    Tunc bibit irriguas fertilis hortus aquas,
Aurea tunc pressos pedibus dedit uva liquores   45
    Mixtaque securo est sobria lympha mero.
Rura ferunt messes, calidi cum sideris aestu
    Deponit flavas annua terra comas.
Rure levis vernos flores apis ingerit alveo,
    Compleat ut dulci sedula melle favos.   50
Agricola assiduo primum satiatus aratro
    Cantavit certo rustica verba pede
Et satur arenti primum est modulatus avena
    Carmen, ut ornatos diceret ante deos,
Agricola et minio suffusus, Bacche, rubenti   55
    Primus inexperta duxit ab arte choros.
Huic datus a pleno, memorabile munus, ovili
    Dux pecoris: curtas auxerat hircus opes.
Rure puer verno primum de flore coronam
    Fecit et antiquis imposuit Laribus.   60
Rure etiam teneris curam exhibitura puellis
    Molle gerit tergo lucida vellus ovis.
Hinc et femineus labor est, hinc pensa colusque,
    Fusus et apposito pollice versat opus,
Atque aliqua assidue textrix operata Minervae   65
    Cantat et appulso tela sonat latere.
Ipse quoque inter agros interque armenta Cupido
    Natus et indomitas dicitur inter equas:

But *Here's to Messalla!* may each and every one say to his cups.
　　Let every word reecho the name of him away.
Messalla, famed for your triumph over the Aquitani,
　　Conqueror, glory of your unshorn forebears,
Be present here, and lend me your spirit while we render　　　　35
　　Thanks to the farmers' deities with our song.
I sing the country and country gods. Taught by them our life
　　Grew unused to banishing hunger with acorns.
They first taught us to build by arrangement of beams,
　　To roof over a tiny house with the green of leaves.　　　　40
And they are said to have first taught bulls to serve
　　Man and to put a wheel beneath the wagon.
Then uncultivated foods were no more. Then fruit was grafted.
　　Then the fertile garden drank the refreshing stream.
Then golden grape yielded drink, crushed by the foot,　　　　45
　　And tempering water was mixed with the carefree wine.
The country bears harvests, and beneath the heat of the burning star
　　The earth at year's fullness sheds its tawny locks.
In the country the nimble bee heaps flowers of spring in the hive,
　　Eager to fill the combs with honey's sweetness.　　　　50
The farmer, surfeited with strenuous work at the plow,
　　First sang country songs to a fixèd beat.
And after meals first tuned a melody on drying reed
　　To sing a song before their honored gods.
And, Bacchus, the farmer full-reddened with vermilion　　　　55
　　First led the dance with skill as yet untrained.
As his gift, notable offering from a full fold, the flock's
　　Lead goat brought increase to a meager stock.
In the country a boy first made a wreath of spring flowers
　　And with it garlanded the ancient Lares.　　　　60
In the country too a gleaming sheep wore on its back a soft fleece,
　　Soon to furnish tasks for our tender girls.
Hence here also women's toil: the wool and the distaff,
　　The spindle turning its work through well-placed thumb.
And some weaver sings ever to Minerva all the while she works　　　　65
　　And causes the loom to rattle as its sides are struck.
Cupid himself also, they say, was born amid the fields,
　　Amid flocks, amid mares left unrestrained.

Illic indocto primum se exercuit arcu:
    Ei mihi, quam doctas nunc habet ille manus!   70
Nec pecudes, velut ante, petit: fixisse puellas
    Gestit et audaces perdomuisse viros.
Hic iuveni detraxit opes, hic dicere iussit
    Limen ad iratae verba pudenda senem:
Hoc duce custodes furtim transgressa iacentes   75
    Ad iuvenem tenebris sola puella venit
Et pedibus praetentat iter suspensa timore,
    Explorat caecas cui manus ante vias.
Ah miseri, quos hic graviter deus urget! at ille
    Felix, cui placidus leniter afflat Amor.   80
Sancte, veni dapibus festis, sed pone sagittas
    Et procul ardentes hinc precor abde faces.
Vos celebrem cantate deum pecorique vocate
    Voce: palam pecori, clam sibi quisque vocet.
Aut etiam sibi quisque palam: iam turba iocosa   85
    Obstrepit et Phrygio tibia curva sono.
Ludite: iam Nox iungit equos currumque sequuntur
    Matris lascivo sidera fulva choro,
Postque venit tacitus furvis circumdatus alis
    Somnus et incerto Somnia nigra pede.   90

2

Dicamus bona verba, venit Natalis ad aras:
    Quisquis ades, lingua, vir mulierque, fave.
Urantur pia tura focis, urantur odores
    Quos tener e terra divite mittit Arabs.
Ipse suos adsit Genius visurus honores,   5
    Cui decorent sanctas mollia serta comas.
Illius puro destillent tempora nardo
    Atque satur libo sit madeatque mero,
Annuat et, Cornute, tibi, quodcumque rogabis.
    En age, quid cessas? annuit ille: roga.   10

2.8: *Atque* for *Aque.*
2.10: *annuit* for *annuet.*

There he first began to train on the untaught bow.
Alas, poor me! How well trained his hands are now!   70
He is not chasing beasts as in the past. Now he aims
To pinion girls and utterly to tame bold men.
He has relieved the youth of his means. He has commanded an elder
to utter
Embarrassing words at an angry woman's door.
He leads the way. A girl alone comes secretly past   75
Her lounging guards in the dark to find her young man.
Frozen by fear she keeps feeling for the path with her feet.
Her hands outstretched in front seek the darkened way.
Ah, poor folk, on whom the god so heavily weighs! But happy
the one
On whom Amor kindly blows his gentle breath.   80
Come, Holy One, to the festive banquet, but set your arrows aside,
And far from here, I pray, shroud your burning torches.
All chant the honored god and call him to the flock! Let each
Sing loudly for the flock, quietly for himself.
Or even sing out loud for himself! Now the playful crowd   85
Roars, and the curved flute in Phrygian tones.
Have your play! Nox now yokes her horses, and the golden stars
Attend their mother's chariot in lusty troop.
Then wrapped in his dark wings Somnus nears
In silence, and black Somnia with unsure tread.   90

2. Cornutus's Birthday

Utter favorable words! Natalis approaches the altar.
Attend, man or woman, with gracious tongue.
Let holy incense burn on the hearth. Let fragrances be burned
That the delicate Arab sends from his rich land.
Let your Genius himself be there to view his honors,   5
His sacred locks crowned with soft garlands.
Let his temples drip with flawless nard.
Let him be glutted with cake and steeped with wine.
And let him nod his support, Cornutus, for whatever you
will request.
Go on! Why hang back? He nods. Make a request!   10

Auguror, uxoris fidos optabis amores:
    Iam reor hoc ipsos edidicisse deos.
Nec tibi malueris, totum quaecumque per orbem
    Fortis arat valido rusticus arva bove,
Nec tibi, gemmarum quidquid felicibus Indis   15
    Nascitur, Eoi qua maris unda rubet.
Vota cadunt. Viden ut strepitantibus advolet alis
    Flavaque coniugio vincula portet Amor,
Vincula quae maneant semper dum tarda senectus
    Inducat rugas inficiatque comas?   20
Huc veniat Natalis avis prolemque ministret,
    Ludat ut ante tuos turba novella pedes.

3

Rura meam, Cornute, tenent villaeque puellam:
    Ferreus est, heu heu, quisquis in urbe manet.
Ipsa Venus laetos iam nunc migravit in agros,
    Verbaque aratoris rustica discit Amor.
O ego, cum aspicerem dominam, quam fortiter illic   5
    Versarem valido pingue bidente solum
Agricolaeque modo curvum sectarer aratrum,
    Dum subigunt steriles arva serenda boves!
Nec quererer, quod sol graciles exureret artus,
    Laederet aut teneras pussula rupta manus.   10
Pavit et Admeti tauros formosus Apollo,
    Nec cithara intonsae profueruntve comae,
Nec potuit curas sanare salubribus herbis:
    Quidquid erat medicae vicerat artis amor.   14
Ipse deus solitus stabulis expellere vaccas   14a
    . . . .
Et miscere novo docuisse coagula lacte,   14b
    Lacteus e mistis obriguisse liquor.   14c
Tunc fiscella levi detexta est vimine iunci,   15
    Raraque per nexus est via facta sero.
O quotiens illo vitulum gestante per agros
    Dicitur occurrens erubuisse soror!

    2.21: *veniat* for *venias; ministret* for *ministres.*

I prophesy your desire: that your wife shall love you truly,
  I think that the gods themselves already knew this.
Nor would you prefer to this any fields of the whole world
  That the strong peasant plows with his stout ox,
Nor prefer whatever jewels come to be among the fertile Indi   15
  Where reddens the wave of the Eoan Sea.
The prayers are cast. Do you see how, flying in on clamorous wings,
  Amor carries yellow bonds for your wedding,
Bonds that may last forever, until sluggish age
  Brings on the wrinkles and bleaches the hair?   20
May Natalis come hither, and to grandparents grant progeny,
  That a fresh young crowd before your feet may play.

3. Nemesis in the Country

The country and its farms have my girl, Cornutus. Sad, yes, sad:
  Whoever stays in town is made of iron.
Now Venus herself has already traveled to the fertile fields,
  And Amor is learning the plowman's country speech.
Ah, if I could only see my lady, how boldly   5
  I would turn the rich soil there with my sturdy hoe,
And just like a farmer I would follow the curved plow
  While oxen furrow the fields for seeds to come.
I would not complain when the sun scorched my slender limbs
  Or a broken blister hurt my delicate hands.   10
Even beautiful Apollo fed Admetus's bulls.
  His lyre and flowing locks were of no avail.
He could not cure his woes with healing herbs.
  Love had conquered his grasp of medical skill.   14
The god himself used to drive the cows from their barns   14a
. . . .
And to have taught how to mix the new milk with rennet   14b
  And the milky liquid to curdle in its pails.   14c
Then a basket was woven with lithe strips of rush,   15
  And through the mesh a thin path formed for whey.
Oh, how often, they say, did his sister blush
  To encounter him lugging a calf through the fields!

O quotiens ausae, caneret cum valle sub alta,
    Rumpere mugitu carmina docta boves!   20
Saepe duces trepidis petiere oracula rebus,
    Venit et a templis irrita turba domum:
Saepe horrere sacros doluit Latona capillos,
    Quos admirata est ipsa noverca prius.
Quisquis inornatumque caput crinesque solutos   25
    Aspiceret, Phoebi quaereret ille comam.
Delos ubi nunc, Phoebe, tua est, ubi Delphica Pytho?
    Nempe Amor in parva te iubet esse casa.
Felices olim, Veneri cum fertur aperte
    Servire aeternos non puduisse deos.   30
Fabula nunc ille est: sed cui sua cura puella est,
    Fabula sit mavult quam sine amore deus.
At tu, quisquis is es, cui tristi fronte Cupido
    Imperat, ut nostra sint tua castra domo,
. . . .

. . . .
Ferrea non Venerem sed praedam saecula laudant: 35
    Praeda tamen multis est operata malis.
Praeda feras acies cinxit discordibus armis:
    Hinc cruor, hinc caedes mors propiorque venit.
Praeda vago iussit geminare pericula ponto,
    Bellica cum dubiis rostra dedit ratibus.   40
Praedator cupit immensos obsidere campos,
    Ut multo innumeram iugere pascat ovem,
Cui lapis externus curae est, urbisque tumultu
    Portatur validis fulta columna iugis,
Claudit et indomitum moles mare, lentus ut intra   45
    Neglegat hibernas piscis adesse minas.
At tibi laeta trahant Samiae convivia testae
    Fictaque Cumana lubrica terra rota.
Heu heu, divitibus video gaudere puellas:
    Iam veniant praedae, si Venus optat opes,   50
Ut mea luxuria Nemesis fluat utque per urbem
    Incedat donis conspicienda meis.
Illa gerat vestes tenues, quas femina Coa
    Texuit, auratas disposuitque vices:

Oh, how often, while he sang in the deep valley, did daring cows
    Break in on his learnèd singing with their moos!   20
Often in times of trial leaders went in search of oracles,
    And from his shrines a thwarted group came home.
Often Latona grieved at the sacred locks in disarray
    That a mother-in-law herself had once admired.
Whoever gazed upon the unadornèd head, the tresses   25
    Loose, would vainly seek for Phoebus's locks.
Phoebus, where is your Delos now, your Delphic Pytho? It is clear:
    Amor orders you to reside in a tiny house.
Happy the days when the undying gods, they say, were not ashamed
    To be slaves of Venus for all to see.   30
Now he's a scandal; yet one with a troublesome girl prefers
    To be a scandal than a loveless god.
But you, whoever you are, whom Cupid, with his countenance severe,
    Orders to set up your camp in our house,

. . . .

    . . . .

Iron ages offer praise to profit, not to Venus,   35
    But profit concerns itself with many an evil.
Profit girded fierce squadrons with hostile arms.
    Then comes blood; then slaughter, and a hasty death.
Profit ordered perils to compound on the roaming sea
    When she gifted unsteady ships with the beaks of war.   40
The profiteer loves to lay siege to enormous tracts of land
    To pasture numberless sheep on many an acre.
If he hankers for imported marble, through the bustling city
    A column is carried, braced on sturdy yokes.
Rock piles enclose the roiling sea so the sluggish fish   45
    Within may pay no heed to winter's threats.
But for you let Samian jugs prolong your happy feasts
    And the wet clay turned on Cumaean wheel.
Alas, alas! I see that girls rejoice in riches.
    Let spoils now come to hand, if Venus craves wealth,   50
That my Nemesis may stream with luxury and through the city
    May process, a cynosure in my gifts.
Let her flaunt gauzy silks, what a woman of Cos
    Has woven and interspersed with veins of gold.

Illi sint comites fusci, quos India torret,   55
   Solis et admotis inficit ignis equis:
Illi selectos certent praebere colores
   Africa puniceum purpureumque Tyros.
Vana loquor: regnum ipse tenet, quem saepe coegit
   Barbara gypsatos ferre catasta pedes.   60
At tibi, dura Ceres, Nemesim quae abducis ab urbe,
   Persolvat nulla semina terra fide.
Et tu, Bacche tener, iucundae consitor uvae,
   Tu quoque devotos, Bacche, relinque lacus.
Haud impune licet formosas tristibus agris   65
   Abdere: non tanti sunt tua musta, pater.
O valeant fruges, ne sint modo rure puellae:
   Glans alat, et prisco more bibantur aquae.
Glans aluit veteres, et passim semper amarunt:
   Quid nocuit sulcos non habuisse satos?   70
Tum, quibus aspirabat Amor, praebebat aperte
   Mitis in umbrosa gaudia valle Venus.
Nullus erat custos, nulla exclusura volentes
   Ianua: si fas est, mos precor ille redi.
. . . .   75
   Horrida villosa corpora veste tegant.
Nunc si clausa mea est, si copia rara videndi,
   Heu miserum, in laxa quid iuvat esse toga?
Ducite: ad imperium dominae sulcabimus agros:
   Non ego me vinclis verberibusque nego.   80

4

Hic mihi servitium video dominamque paratam:
   Iam mihi, libertas illa paterna, vale.
Servitium sed triste datur, teneorque catenis,
   Et nunquam misero vincla remittit Amor,
Et seu quid merui seu nil peccavimus, urit.   5
   Uror io: remove, saeva puella, faces.

Let her have darkened slaves whom India scalds   55
    And the sun's fire dyes as his horses approach nearby.
Let Africa and Tyros vie in offering her
    A choice of hues, bright crimson and violet.
My words are useless. He holds sway whom the platform
      for barbarians
    Often compelled to shuffle his gypsumed feet.   60
But for you, hard Ceres, who lure Nemesis away from the city,
    May earth faithlessly fail to repay your seed.
And you, tender Bacchus, planter of the pleasant grape,
    You also, Bacchus, abandon your cursèd vats.
You will pay for concealing beauty in wretched fields.   65
    Your new wine, Father, is not worth that much.
Fare you well, O crops, so no girls are in the country. As of old,
    Let acorns be our food, and water our drink.
Acorns fed the ancients, and they made love ever and everywhere.
    What harm did the lack of seeded furrows do?   70
Then to those Amor favored gentle Venus openly
    Granted her delights in shady valley.
There was no guard, no doorway to shut out the eager.
    Old custom, if I may, please do return.
. . . .   75
    Let them cover their uncouth limbs with shaggy pelt.
Now if my girl is shut away and I have no chance to see her,
    Alas, what pleasure for sad me in a flowing toga?
Lead on! At our lady's command we will furrow our lands.
    I will not say no to chains and to the lash.   80

4. At Nemesis's Doorway

So my gaze is on slavery and a lady ready to rule.
    Fare you well, freedom that was my fathers'.
But bitter slavery is my lot, and I am bound in chains.
    And in my sorrow Amor never loosens the bonds.
And whether I have deserved it or sinned not at all, he burns.   5
    Yes, I am on fire. Cruel girl, take away your torches.

O ego ne possim tales sentire dolores,
    Quam mallem in gelidis montibus esse lapis,
Stare vel insanis cautes obnoxia ventis,
    Naufraga quam vasti tunderet unda maris!   10
Nunc et amara dies et noctis amarior umbra est:
    Omnia nam tristi tempora felle madent.
Nec prosunt elegi nec carminis auctor Apollo:
    Illa cava pretium flagitat usque manu.
Ite procul, Musae, si non prodestis amanti: 15
    Non ego vos, ut sint bella canenda, colo,
Nec refero solisque vias nec qualis, ubi orbem
    Complevit, versis Luna recurrit equis.
Ad dominam faciles aditus per carmina quaero:
    Ite procul, Musae, si nihil ista valent.   20
Aut mihi per caedem et facinus sunt dona paranda,
    Ne iaceam clausam flebilis ante domum
Aut rapiam suspensa sacris insignia fanis:
    Sed Venus ante alios est violanda mihi.
Illa malum facinus suadet dominamque rapacem   25
    Dat mihi: sacrilegas sentiat illa manus.
O pereat, quicumque legit viridesque smaragdos
    Et niveam Tyrio murice tingit ovem.
Addit avaritiae causas et Coa puellis
    Vestis et e rubro lucida concha mari.   30
Haec fecere malas: hinc clavim ianua sensit
    Et coepit custos liminis esse canis.
Sed, pretium si grande feras, custodia victa est
    Nec prohibent claves, et canis ipse tacet.
Heu, quicumque dedit formam caelestis avarae,   35
    Quale bonum multis addidit ille malis!
Hinc fletus rixaeque sonant, haec denique causa
    Fecit ut infamis nunc deus erret Amor.
At tibi, quae pretio victos excludis amantes,
    Diripiant partas ventus et ignis opes: 40
Quin tua tunc iuvenes spectent incendia laeti,
    Nec quisquam flammae sedulus addat aquam,
Seu veniet tibi mors, neque sit qui lugeat ullus,
    Nec qui det maestas munus in exsequias.

Oh, for me to be able to dull such sufferings,
    I would rather be a rock on the frozen mountains
Or stand as a crag opposing maddened winds,
    That a ship-breaking wave batters on the boundless sea.   10
And now the day is bitter; night's shadow, more bitter still.
    For every moment is steeped in the gloom of gall.
Elegies do no good, nor Apollo, the creator of song.
    She ever demands her price with hollowed hand.
Away, Muses, far off, if you are no help to lovers!   15
    I worship you not to sing of wars,
Not to sing of the sun's paths, nor how, with her course completed,
    Luna arrives with her steeds turned around.
Through songs I ask easy access to my mistress.
    Away, Muses, far off, if they have no power.   20
Either I must gather gifts by way of mayhem and crime,
    Lest I lie in tears before her closèd door,
Or I will steal emblems hanging in holy shrines.
    But I must desecrate Venus before the rest.
She urges the evil of crime and gives me a greedy mistress: 25
    Let her feel the touch of my profane hands.
A curse on him who searches out shining emeralds
    And who dyes the snowy fleece with Tyrian purple.
Coan cloth inflames young girls with greed
    And the shining conch from a crimson sea.   30
These turned them evil. As a result the door felt a key,
    And a dog began to keep guard at the threshold.
But if you carry a huge price, the guardian's care lapses away;
    The keys fail to work; the dog itself keeps still.
Alas, whichever god thought to unite beauty with greed: 35
    What sort of good did he attach to a mass of evil!
Hence sobs and shrieks reecho. This in fact was the reason
    Why the ill-famed god Amor now roams abroad.
But you who shut out lovers whose price falls short,
    May wind and fire ruin your amassèd wealth.   40
Yes, let youths with joy then observe the flames at work,
    Nor let some kindly person douse the blaze.
But if your death draw near, may there be no one to mourn
    Nor to bestow a gift at your sad funeral rites.

At bona quae nec avara fuit, centum licet annos 45
    Vixerit, ardentem flebitur ante rogum:
Atque aliquis senior veteres veneratus amores
    Annua constructo serta dabit tumulo
Et 'bene' discedens dicet 'placideque quiescas,
    Terraque securae sit super ossa levis.' 50
Vera quidem moneo, sed prosunt quid mihi vera?
    Illius est nobis lege colendus Amor.
Quin etiam sedes iubeat si vendere avitas,
    Ite sub imperium sub titulumque, Lares.
Quidquid habet Circe, quidquid Medea veneni, 55
    Quidquid et herbarum Thessala terra gerit,
Et quod, ubi indomitis gregibus Venus afflat amores,
    Hippomanes cupidae stillat ab inguine equae,
Si modo me placido videat Nemesis mea vultu,
    Mille alias herbas misceat illa, bibam. 60

5

Phoebe, fave: novus ingreditur tua templa sacerdos:
    Huc age cum cithara carminibusque veni.
Nunc te vocales impellere pollice chordas,
    Nunc precor ad laudis flectere verba modos.
Ipse triumphali devinctus tempora lauro, 5
    Dum cumulant aras, ad tua sacra veni.
Sed nitidus pulcherque veni: nunc indue vestem
    Sepositam, longas nunc bene pecte comas,
Qualem te memorant Saturno rege fugato
    Victori laudes concinuisse Iovi. 10
Tu procul eventura vides, tibi deditus augur
    Scit bene quid fati provida cantet avis,
Tuque regis sortes, per te praesentit aruspex,
    Lubrica signavit cum deus exta notis,
Te duce Romanos nunquam frustrata Sibylla est 15
    Abdita quae senis fata canit pedibus.

But a good woman, stranger to greed, though she live a
     hundred years,   45
    Will receive our tears before her burning pyre.
And some aged man, in honor of love's long span,
    Will place a wreath each year on the heaped-up tomb
And parting he will say: *Sleep quietly and well,*
    And may earth lie lightly on your tranquil bones.   50
Surely my warnings are true, but what good are truths to me?
    Our Amor must be worshipped according to her rules.
Even if her order says sell the ancestral estate,
    Lares, submit to her will and her command.
Whatever poisons Circe or Medea controls, whatever   55
    Herbs the land of Thessaly brings forth,
And, when Venus incites the untamed herds to love,
    What horse-madness drips from the groin of a lusting mare,
If but once Nemesis would glance at me with gentle wink,
    Though she mingle a thousand diverse herbs, I will drink.   60

5. The Initiation of Messallinus

Phoebus, bless us. A new priest enters your temple.
    Come to us, here and now, with lyre and song.
Now strike the melodious strings with your thumb, I pray:
    Now turn my words to the tunes of praise.
And with your brow bound with a triumph's laurel,   5
    While they heap your altars, come, yourself, to your rites.
But come, shimmering and beautiful. Don, now, this raiment
    Long set aside. Now comb well your streaming locks,
As in that time when, after King Saturn's rout,
    They recall you sang out the glory of conquering Jove.   10
From afar you see the future. The augur in your service
    Well understands what fates the prophetic bird sings.
You control the lots. Through you the diviner foresees
    When the god with his signs has marked the sleek entrails.
And, following your lead, the Sibyl, who never has deceived
     the Romans,   15
    Sings profound predictions in six-foot lines.

Phoebe, sacras Messalinum sine tangere chartas
    Vatis, et ipse precor quid canat illa doce.
Haec dedit Aeneae sortes, postquam ille parentem
    Dicitur et raptos sustinuisse Lares.   20
(Nec fore credebat Romam, cum maestus ab alto
    Ilion ardentes respiceretque deos:
Romulus aeternae nondum formaverat urbis
    Moenia, consorti non habitanda Remo,
Sed tunc pascebant herbosa Palatia vaccae   25
    Et stabant humiles in Iovis arce casae.
Lacte madens illic suberat Pan ilicis umbrae
    Et facta agresti lignea falce Pales,
Pendebatque vagi pastoris in arbore votum,
    Garrula silvestri fistula sacra deo,   30
Fistula cui semper decrescit arundinis ordo,
    Nam calamus cera iungitur usque minor.
At qua Velabri regio patet, ire solebat
    Exiguus pulsa per vada linter aqua.
Illac saepe gregis diti placitura magistro   35
    Ad iuvenem festa est vecta puella die,
Cum qua fecundi redierunt munera ruris,
    Caseus et niveae candidus agnus ovis.)
'Impiger Aenea, volitantis frater Amoris,
    Troica qui profugis sacra vehis ratibus,   40
Iam tibi Laurentes assignat Iuppiter agros,
    Iam vocat errantes hospita terra Lares.
Illic sanctus eris, cum te veneranda Numici
    Unda deum caelo miserit Indigetem.
Ecce super fessas volitans Victoria puppes   45
    Tandem ad Troianos diva superba venit.
Ecce mihi lucent Rutulis incendia castris:
    Iam tibi praedico, barbare Turne, necem.
Ante oculos Laurens castrum murusque Lavini est
    Albaque ab Ascanio condita Longa duce.   50
Te quoque iam video, Marti placitura sacerdos
    Ilia, Vestales deseruisse focos,

5.23: *formaverat* for *firmaverat*.
5.50: *Longa* for *longa*.

Phoebus, permit Messallinus to touch the seer's holy books;
  Yourself, I pray, expound to him what she sings.
She gave a prophecy to Aeneas after, it is said,
  He had shouldered his father and his rescued gods.   20
(For, grieving, he failed to believe in a future Rome as from the sea
  He cast his eye back at Ilion and its gods aflame.
Romulus had not yet shaped the eternal city's walls,
  Never to be the home of Remus, his twin.
At that time cows cropped the grassy Palatium   25
  And lowly huts stood on Jove's citadel.
Pan, dripping with milk, took shade there under an oak,
  And a wooden Pales was fashioned with rustic hook,
And the chattering pipe, sacred to the sylvan god, was hanging
  On a tree, a wandering shepherd's offering,   30
A pipe of reed arranged in ever-decreasing slant,
  For each still smaller stalk is joined with wax.
And, where the Velabrum opens out, a slender skiff used to
  Glide an oar-struck pathway through the waves.
There often on a festal day a girl journeyed to her lover,   35
  To be the pleasure of the rich owner of the herd.
With her returned the produce of the fertile country,
  Cheese and a shining lamb from a snowy sheep.)
"Untiring Aeneas, brother of wingèd Amor,
  Who carry Troy's holy objects on ships of exile,   40
Now Jove marks out the Laurentian fields for you.
  Now a welcoming land beckons your wandering Lares.
And there you will become venerated when the holy wave
  Of the Numicus will send you to heaven as Indiges.
Look how Victoria, soaring above your exhausted fleet,   45
  Comes a proud goddess to the Trojans at long last.
Look! I see fires gleam in the Rutulian camp.
  And now, savage Turnus, I predict your death.
Before my eyes are the Laurentian camp and the Lavinian wall
  And Alba Longa founded by Lord Ascanius.   50
And you, Priestess, I see have abandoned Vesta's hearth,
  Ilia, now ready to be the pleasure of Mars,

Concubitusque tuos furtim vittasque iacentes
    Et cupidi ad ripas arma relicta dei.
Carpite nunc, tauri, de septem montibus herbas   55
    Dum licet: hic magnae iam locus urbis erit.
Roma, tuum nomen terris fatale regendis,
    Qua sua de caelo prospicit arva Ceres,
Quaque patent ortus et qua fluitantibus undis
    Solis anhelantes abluit amnis equos.   60
Troia quidem tunc se mirabitur et sibi dicet
    Vos bene tam longa consuluisse via.
Vera cano: sic usque sacras innoxia laurus
    Vescar, et aeternum sit mihi virginitas.'
Haec cecinit vates et te sibi, Phoebe, vocavit,   65
    Iactavit fusa et caput ante coma.
Quicquid Amalthea, quicquid Marpesia dixit
    Herophile, Phoeto Graia quod admonuit,
Quotque Aniena sacras Tiburs per flumina sortes
    Portarat sicco pertuleratque sinu   70
(Haec fore dixerunt, belli mala signa, cometen,
    Multus ut in terras deplueretque lapis
Atque tubas atque arma ferunt crepitantia caelo
    Audita et lucos praecinuisse fugam.
Ipsum etiam Solem defectum lumine vidit   75
    Iungere pallentes nubilus annus equos.
Et simulacra deum lacrimas fudisse tepentes
    Fataque vocales praemonuisse boves.)
Haec fuerant olim, sed tu, iam mitis, Apollo,
    Prodigia indomitis merge sub aequoribus   80
Et succensa sacris crepitet bene laurea flammis
    Omine quo felix et satur annus erit.
Laurus ubi bona signa dedit (gaudete coloni),
    Distendet spicis horrea plena Ceres
Oblitus et musto feriet pede rusticus uvas,   85
    Dolia dum magni deficiantque lacus,

5.67: *Amalthea* for *Amalthee; Marpesia* for *Mermessia.*
5.68: *Graia quod admonuit* for *Graiaque quod monuit.*
5.74–79: Text and translation follow the line order of the manuscripts.
5.79: *fuerant* for *fuerint.*

Your secret trysts, virgin's ribbons flung aside, the armor
    Of the ardent god abandoned at the banks.
Now while you may, bulls, feed on the grass of the Seven Hills.   55
    Presently a great city will arise here.
Rome, your name strikes awe in the countries you will rule,
    Where Ceres gazes down from heaven upon her fields,
Where Sol's risings open, and where the Ocean stream washes
    His breathless horses in its rushing waves.   60
Then Troy for sure will marvel at herself and will say
    That you looked after her well on the long, long road.
I sing the truth: so may I ever feed on blessèd laurel
    Without harm, and remain a virgin for all time."
Thus sang the priestess and, Phoebus, she called you to her,   65
    Tossing her head as her hair fell across her face.
Whatever Amalthea said, whatever Marpesian Herophile,
    And what Graian Phoeto had forewarned,
As many sacred lots as Anian Tiburs carried through
    And brought out from the stream, her clothes still dry: 70
These told of a future comet, war's dire sign,
    How a shower of rock rained onto earth
And, they say, trumpets and weapons were heard clashing
    In the sky, and groves sang of flight to come.
And a year of clouds saw even the light fail   75
    Of Sol himself, as he yoked his sallow steeds.
Statues of the gods bathed in warm tears,
    And talking cattle forewarned what lay ahead.
This happened once upon a time; but Apollo, now merciful,
    Please drown these portents in the untamed sea,   80
And let the kindled laurel crackle kindly in the holy fire—
    An omen for a year to be glad and full.
And—Farmers, rejoice!—when the laurel has given auspicious signs,
    Ceres will stretch the barns brim-full with corn.
And the peasant will tread grapes with must-soaked feet   85
    While jugs and great vats still have space to spare.

Ac madidus Baccho sua festa Parilia pastor
    Concinet: a stabulis tunc procul este, lupi.
Ille levis stipulae sollemnis potus acervos
    Accendet, flammas transilietque sacras,   90
Et fetus matrona dabit, natusque parenti
    Oscula comprensis auribus eripiet,
Nec taedebit avum parvo advigilare nepoti
    Balbaque cum puero dicere verba senem.
Tunc operata deo pubes discumbet in herba,   95
    Arboris antiquae qua levis umbra cadit,
Aut e veste sua tendent umbracula sertis
    Vincta, coronatus stabit et ipse calix,
Aut sibi quisque dapes et festas extruet alte
    Caespitibus mensas caespitibusque torum.   100
Ingeret hic potus iuvenis maledicta puellae,
    Post modo quae votis irrita facta velit:
Nam ferus ille suae plorabit sobrius idem
    Et se iurabit mente fuisse mala.
Pace tua pereant arcus pereantque sagittae,   105
    Phoebe, modo in terris erret inermis Amor.
Ars bona: sed postquam sumpsit sibi tela Cupido,
    Heu heu, quam multis ars dedit ista malum!
Et mihi praecipue: iaceo dum saucius annum
    Et faveo morbo quem iuvat ipse dolor,   110
Usque cano Nemesim, sine qua versus mihi nullus
    Verba potest iustos aut reperire pedes.
At tu (nam divum servat tutela poetas)
    Praemoneo, vati parce, puella, sacro,
Ut Messalinum celebrem cum, praemia belli,   115
    Ante suos currus oppida victa ferent,
Ipse gerens laurus, lauro devinctus agresti,
    Miles 'io' magna voce 'triumphe' canet.
Tunc Messalla meus pia det spectacula turbae
    Et plaudat curru praetereunte pater.   120
Annue: sic tibi sint intonsi, Phoebe, capilli,
    Sic tua perpetuo sit tibi casta soror.

5.118: *canet* for *canam*.

And the shepherd, steeped in Bacchus, will sing the festive
    Parilia. Then, wolves, keep far from the pens.
Drunk now, he will kindle the holy piles of light straw,
    And then he will leap across the blessèd flames.   90
Then his wife will give birth, and a son will steal kisses
    From his father, seizing him by the ears.
It will not trouble grandfather to watch small grandchild
    Or at his age to prattle at the boy.
Then, having worshiped the god, the young will recline on
      the grass   95
    Where a light shadow falls from an ancient tree.
Or from their garments they will stretch small awnings adorned
      with wreaths,
    And the mixing bowl itself will display a crown.
Or each will set up his feast for himself, and festive tables
    On high turf, and couches out of turf.   100
And a drunken youth will hurl curses on his girl
    That afterward he may wish he had prayed in vain.
For sober he will weep that he was fierce to her,
    And he will swear that he had been out of his mind.
Phoebus, if you will, may your bows perish; perish your arrows   105
    So that Amor unarmed may roam the earth.
Your skill is good, but after Cupid took up weapons for himself,
    Alas! Alas, to how many that art brought harm!
And mainly to me. I lie wounded the entire year,
    And I nurture the disease that grief itself supplies: 110
I sing without stop of Nemesis, without whom no line,
    No word of mine, can discover its proper beat.
But you, my girl—for poets are under the gods' protection—
    I earnestly advise, spare the holy bard
That I might honor Messallinus when, before his chariot   115
    They will carry conquered towns, the spoils of war.
Wearing the laurel, crowned with the rustic laurel, the soldiers
    Themselves will shout *Hail, Triumph!* in full voice.
Then let my Messalla sponsor entertainment for the crowd,
    And, as father, applaud when the chariot passes by.   120
Phoebus, say yes. Thus may your locks forever flow long.
    And your sister be eternally chaste—thus my song.

Castra Macer sequitur: tenero quid fiet Amori?
  Sit comes et collo fortiter arma gerat?
Et seu longa virum terrae via seu vaga ducent
  Aequora, cum telis ad latus ire volet?
Ure, puer, quaeso, tua qui ferus otia liquit,   5
  Atque iterum erronem sub tua signa voca.
Quod si militibus parces, erit hic quoque miles,
  Ipse levem galea qui sibi portet aquam.
Castra peto, valeatque Venus valeantque puellae:
  Et mihi sunt vires et mihi flata tuba est.   10
Magna loquor, sed magnifice mihi magna locuto
  Excutiunt clausae fortia verba fores.
Iuravi quotiens rediturum ad limina nunquam!
  Cum bene iuravi, pes tamen ipse redit.
Acer Amor, fractas utinam, tua tela, sagittas,   15
  Si licet, extinctas aspiciamque faces!
Tu miserum torques, tu me mihi dira precari
  Cogis et insana mente nefanda loqui.
Iam mala finissem leto, sed credula vitam
  Spes fouet et fore cras semper ait melius.   20
Spes alit agricolas, Spes sulcis credit aratis
  Semina, quae magno faenore reddat ager:
Haec laqueo volucres, haec captat harundine pisces,
  Cum tenues hamos abdidit ante cibus:
Spes etiam valida solatur compede vinctum: 25
  (Crura sonant ferro, sed canit inter opus)
Spes facilem Nemesim spondet mihi, sed negat illa.
  Ei mihi, ne vincas, dura puella, deam.
Parce, per immatura tuae precor ossa sororis:
  Sic bene sub tenera parva quiescat humo.   30
Illa mihi sancta est, illius dona sepulcro
  Et madefacta meis serta feram lacrimis:
Illius ad tumulum fugiam supplexque sedebo
  Et mea cum muto fata querar cinere.

6. At Nemesis's Doorway—Again

Macer is going to war. What will become of gentle Amor? Should he
    Follow along and boldly shoulder his gear?
Whether land's long route or wandering seas will lead his way,
    Will Amor wish with weapons to follow by his side?
Set him afire I pray, boy—he has wildly abandoned your life
        of ease—   5
    And call the deserter back under your flag.
But if you are kindly to soldiers, then he will also be a soldier
    Himself, to carry in his helmet shifting water's draft.
I am going to war. Venus, goodbye! Goodbye, girls!
    The strength is mine; the trumpet blows for me.   10
My speech is grand; yet, though my eloquence be grand,
    Closed doors shunt back to me my mighty words.
How many times have I sworn I would never go back to that
        threshold.
    My oath sounded fine, but of itself my foot returns.
Harsh Amor, would that I may behold arrows   15
    Broken—those weapons of yours—and torches doused!
You torture the lovesick. You drive me to curse myself
    And to utter the unspeakable from a mind gone far astray.
I would have ended my woes in death save that trustful Spes ever
    Fosters life and promises a better day.   20
Spes feeds the farmers. Spes entrusts to the plowed furrows
    Seeds the field returns with plentiful interest.
She catches birds with the snare and fish with the rod,
    When the bait has served to hide the slender hooks.
Spes also consoles a man bound in heavy chains—his shins   25
    Resound from the metal, but he sings amid his tasks.
Spes assures me a yielding Nemesis; but she says no.
    Watch out, hard girl! Do not attempt to outdo a goddess!
Have pity, I pray, by the bones of your small sister, early to die.
    May she rest quietly beneath the gentle ground.   30
I hold her sacred. I will carry to her grave
    Gifts and wreaths all sodden from my tears.
I will take refuge at her tomb, and I will sit there, a suppliant,
    And moan about my fate to the voiceless ash.

Non feret usque suum te propter flere clientem: 35
    Illius ut verbis, sis mihi lenta veto,
Ne tibi neglecti mittant mala somnia Manes,
    Maestaque sopitae stet soror ante torum,
Qualis ab excelsa praeceps delapsa fenestra
    Venit ad infernos sanguinolenta lacus.   40
Desino, ne dominae luctus renoventur acerbi:
    Non ego sum tanti, ploret ut illa semel
Nec lacrimis oculos digna est foedare loquaces:
    Lena nocet nobis, ipsa puella bona est.
Lena necat miserum Phryne furtimque tabellas   45
    Occulto portans itque reditque sinu:
Saepe, ego cum dominae dulces a limine duro
    Agnosco voces, haec negat esse domi:
Saepe, ubi nox promissa mihi est, languere puellam
    Nuntiat aut aliquas extimuisse minas.   50
Tunc morior curis, tunc mens mihi perdita fingit,
    Quisve meam teneat, quot teneatve modis:
Tunc tibi, lena, precor diras: satis anxia vives,
    Moverit e votis pars quotacumque deos.

6.45: *Phryne* for *recipi*.

She will not endure having her devotee ever weeping over you.
      I forbid   35
   Indifference to her words, indifference toward me
Lest her neglected Manes send you evil dreams, and your sister
   Stand sad before your bed as you lie asleep,
As she was when she slipped from the high window
   And made her way, blood-smeared, to the lakes below.   40
I will stop now lest my lady's bitter grief be renewed.
   My worth is not so great that she cry even once,
Nor does she deserve to stain her eloquent eyes with tears.
   The bawd does us harm. The girl herself is good.
The bawd Phryne does me in, poor me, as she slyly comes and goes,   45
   Carrying missives hidden in her garment's folds.
Often, when I take in my mistress's sweet tones
   From the hard door, she says that she is not at home.
Often when I am promised a night, she informs me
   That the girl is sick or terrorized by threats.   50
Worries kill me. Then my ruined mind imagines
   Who holds my love, who holds and in what ways.
And so, bawd, I pray the Furies: your life will be filled with travail,
   Should a small part of my prayers to the gods avail.

Lygdamus

Corpus Tibullianum: Liber Tertius, 1–6

I

Martis Romani festae venere kalendae
  (Exoriens nostris hic fuit annus avis),
Et vaga nunc certa discurrunt undique pompa
  Perque vias urbis munera perque domos:
Dicite, Pierides, quonam donetur honore   5
  Seu mea, seu fallor, cara Neaera tamen.
'Carmine formosae, pretio capiuntur avarae:
  Gaudeat, ut digna est, versibus illa tuis.
Lutea sed niveum involvat membrana libellum,
  Pumex et canas tondeat ante comas,   10
Summaque praetexat tenuis fastigia chartae
  Indicet ut nomen littera facta tuum,
Atque inter geminas pingantur cornua frontes:
  Sic etenim comptum mittere oportet opus.'
Per vos, auctores huius mihi carminis, oro   15
  Castaliamque undam Pieriosque lacus,
Ite domum cultumque illi donate libellum,
  Sicut erit: nullus defluat inde color.
Illa mihi referet, sit nostri mutua cura
  An minor, an toto pectore deciderim.   20
Sed primum meritam larga donate salute
  Atque haec submisso dicite verba sono:

1.3: *certa* for *crebra.*
1.10: *et* for *cui.*
1.11: *chartae* for *charta.*
1.12: *facta* for *picta.*
1.13: *inter* for *infra.*

Lygdamus

Corpus Tibullianum 3.1–6

1. A Gift for Neaera

The festive Kalends of Roman Mars have come
   (Here for our ancestors the year began),
And through the city's streets and homes in orderly parade
   Everywhere gifts hurry, now there, now here.
Pierians, tell me: What offering will we present Neaera,   5
   Dear to me still, whether mine or she plays me false?
"Beautiful girls are snared by song; greedy ones, by cash.
   As she deserves, let her take pleasure in your verses.
But let yellow parchment wrap the gleaming volume,
   And first let pumice trim its whitening locks,   10
And may writing fashioned to declare your name
   Fringe the thin papyrus's peaked tops.
And let the knobs be painted between both its brows,
   For thus it's right to send your well-wrought work."
By the spring of Castalia and Pierian pools,   15
   I pray you, as the begetters of this my song:
Off to her house! Present the smart little volume
   Just as it is! Let none of its glow fade away.
To me she will respond, whether our love be as one, or lessened,
   Or if I have fallen fully from her heart.   20
First greet her deservedly, with ample bow,
   And speak these words in gently voicèd tones:

'Haec tibi vir quondam, nunc frater, casta Neaera,
    Mittit et accipias munera parva rogat,
Teque suis iurat caram magis esse medullis,   25
    Sive sibi coniunx sive futura soror;
Sed potius coniunx: huius spem nominis illi
    Auferet extincto pallida Ditis aqua.'

2

Qui primus caram iuveni carumque puellae
    Eripuit iuvenem, ferreus ille fuit.
Durus et ille fuit, qui tantum ferre dolorem,
    Vivere et erepta coniuge qui potuit.
Non ego firmus in hoc, non haec patientia nostro   5
    Ingenio: frangit fortia corda dolor.
Nec mihi vera loqui pudor est vitaeque fateri
    Tot mala perpessae taedia nota meae.
Ergo ego cum tenuem fuero mutatus in umbram
    Candidaque ossa supra nigra favilla teget,   10
Ante meum veniat longos incompta capillos
    Et fleat ante meum maesta Neaera rogum.
Sed veniat carae matris comitata dolore:
    Maereat haec genero, maereat illa viro.
Praefatae ante meos Manes animamque precatae   15
    Perfusaeque pias ante liquore manus,
Pars quae sola mei superabit corporis, ossa
    Incinctae nigra candida veste legent
Et primum annoso spargant collecta Lyaeo,
    Mox etiam niveo lacte parent,   20
Post haec carbaseis humorem tollere velis
    Atque in marmorea ponere sicca domo.
'Illuc quas mittit dives Panchaia merces
    Eoique Arabes, dives et Assyria,
Et nostri memores lacrimae fundantur eodem: 25
    Sic ego componi versus in ossa velim.

"Your lover once, your brother now, chaste Neaera, sends you
    These tiny gifts and asks that you take them in.
He swears you are dearer to him than his heart and soul,
    Whether you will be his sister or his wife.
But rather his wife! Hope for this title only will Dis's
    Sallow waters take away when he dies."

2. The Poet's Funeral

He was a man of iron who first carried off a dear girl
    From her boy, and a dear boy from her girl.
He was a man of stone who, with his wife snatched away,
    Was able to withstand such grief and survive.
In this I am not sturdy. Nor is this steadiness   5
    In my blood. Grief breaks the brave of heart.
Nor am I ashamed to speak the truth and to admit my loathing
    Of a life that has endured so many woes.
So when I will be transformed into a wisp of shade
    And my white bones black ash will overlay,   10
Let Neaera come to face my pyre, her long hair in disarray.
    Let her weep in sadness as she faces it.
Let her come companioned by her dear mother's grief.
    One mourns a son-in-law; the other a husband mourns.
First they address my Manes and, with prayer, my soul;   15
    First they purify their hands in water's bath;
Ungirdled, in robes of black, they gather my white bones—
    My body's only remnant to survive.
Let them first sprinkle what they have gathered with
        mellow Lyaeus,
    Ready soon also to pour out snowy milk,   20
Afterwards to blot up the moisture with linen cloths,
    And bury them, dry, in their marble dwelling place.
Thereon let the yield that rich Panchaia sends,
    And the Eoan Arabes and rich Assyria,
And tears in our memory be shed right then and there.   25
    Thus, now turned to bone, I want to be buried.

Sed tristem mortis demonstret littera causam
    Atque haec in celebri carmina fronte notet:
'Lygdamus hic situs est: dolor huic et cira Neaerae,
    Coniugis ereptae, causa perire fui.'   30

3

Quid prodest caelum votis implesse, Neaera,
    Blandaque cum multa tura dedisse prece?
Non ut marmorei prodirem e limine tecti,
    Insignis clara conspicuusque domo
Aut ut multa mei renovarent iugera tauri   5
    Et magnas messes terra benigna daret,
Sed tecum ut longae sociarem gaudia vitae
    Inque tuo caderet nostra senecta sinu
Tum cum permenso defunctus tempore lucis
    Nudus Lethaea cogerer ire rate.   10
Nam grave quid prodest pondus mihi divitis auri,
    Arvaque si findant pinguia mille boves?
Quidve domus prodest Phrygiis innixa columnis,
    Taenare sive tuis, sive Caryste tuis,
Et nemora in domibus sacros imitantia lucos   15
    Aurataeque trabes marmoreumque solum?
Quidve in Erythraeo legitur quae litore concha
    Tinctaque Sidonio murice lana iuvat,
Et quae praeterea populus miratur? in illis
    Invidia est: falso plurima vulgus amat.   20
Non opibus mentes hominum curaeque levantur:
    Nam Fortuna sua tempora lege regit.
Sit mihi paupertas tecum iucunda, Neaera:
    At sine te regum munera nulla volo.
O niveam, quae te poterit mihi reddere, lucem!   25
    O mihi felicem terque quaterque diem!
At si, pro dulci reditu quaecumque voventur,
    Audiat aversa non meus aure deus,
Nec me regna iuvant nec Lydius aurifer amnis
    Nec quas terrarum sustinet orbis opes.   30

But let writing testify to my death's sad cause
    And with these lines engrave for all to see:
Here Lygdamus lies. His cause of death was grief,
    Of his wife, Neaera, painfully bereft.   30

3. The Return of Neaera

What help, Neaera, to have glutted the heavens with vows
    And to have offered winning incense with many a prayer,
Not that I might step forth from the threshold of a marble dwelling,
    Illustrious and famed for my resplendent house,
Or that bulls of mine plow anew many an acre   5
    And the kindly earth bestow grand harvests
But that I might share with you the joys of a long life
    And in your lap my old age fall to end
Then, when with the completion of my light's full time,
    Naked I'd have to travel on Lethe's boat.   10
What help to me is gold's heavy weight of riches
    Or a thousand oxen furrowing fertile fields?
What help a house supported on Phrygian columns,
    Or, Taenarus, yours, or yours, Carystus, too,
And within my dwelling woods that resemble sacred groves,   15
    And gilded beams, and a pavement made of marble?
What help the pearl shell gathered on Erythraea's shore,
    Or wool soaked in Sidon's purple dye,
And whatever else the crowd admires? This way lies envy.
    The mob errs in most of what it loves.   20
Men's schemes and worries are not relieved by wealth;
    For Fortuna rules their lives by her own law.
With you, Neaera, poverty would be sweet for me.
    Without you I do not want the opulence of kings.
Oh, snow-bright morning that can return you back to me!   25
    Oh, day, happy for me, threefold, fourfold!
But if a hostile god should fail to hear, ear ill disposed,
    Whatever I have vowed for your sweet return,
Neither kingdoms please me, nor Lydia's gold-filled stream,
    Nor the wealth the circle of the world supports.   30

Haec alii cupiant: liceat mihi paupere cultu
    Securo cara coniuge posse frui.
Adsis et timidis faveas, Saturnia, votis,
    Et faveas concha, Cypria, vecta tua.
Aut si fata negant reditum tristesque sorores,   35
    Stamina quae ducunt quaeque futura neunt,
Me vocet in vastos amnes nigramque paludem
    Dives in ignava luridus Orcus aqua.

4

Di meliora ferant, nec sint mihi somnia vera,
    Quae tulit hesterna pessima nocte quies.
Ite procul, vani. Falsumque avertite visum:
    Desinite in nobis quaerere velle fidem.
Divi vera monent, venturae nuntia sortis   5
    Vera monent Tuscis exta probata viris;
Somnia fallaci ludunt temeraria nocte
    Et pavidas mentes falsa timere iubent,
Et natum in curas hominum genus omina noctis
    Farre pio placant et saliente sale!   10
Et tamen, utcumque est, sive illi vera moneri,
    Mendaci somno credere sive volent,
Efficiat vanos noctis Lucina timores
    Et frustra immeritum pertimuisse velit,
Si mea nec turpi mens est obnoxia facto   15
    Nec laesit magnos impia lingua deos.
Iam Nox aetherium nigris emensa quadrigis
    Mundum caeruleo laverat amne rotas,
Nec me sopierat menti deus utilis aegrae,
    Somnus sollicitas deficit ante domos.   20
Tandem, cum summo Phoebus prospexit ab ortu,
    Pressit languentis lumina sera quies.
Hic iuvenis casta redimitus tempora lauro
    Est visus nostra ponere sede pedem.

3.38: *dives in ignava . . . aqua* for *dis et in ignaram . . . aquam.*
4.1: *mihi somnia* for *insomnia.*
4.3: *vani* for *vanum est.*
4.20: *deficit ante* for *deserit ille.*

Let others yearn for these. Let me but live in poor man's style,
    To enjoy without worry the dearness of my wife.
Stay near, Saturnia, kindly to my fearful prayers,
    Kindly, too, Cypria, traveling on your shell.
But if the Fates deny your return, and the drear sisters   35
    Who draw out our threads and spin our destiny,
May wan Orcus, rich with languorous waters, summon me
    Toward his dreary streams and dusky mere.

4. An Epiphany of Apollo

May the gods provide better! May my dreams not prove true,
    Which sleep at its ugliest brought to me last night!
Off far away, delusive visions! Turn falsehood away!
    Cease to want to gain credit at our expense!
The gods send true warnings; true warnings the entrails, approved   5
    By Tuscan seers, heralding imminent fate.
But dreams mock rashly in the deceiving night
    And order our shuddering minds to feel false fears,
And the race of men, inclined to worry, conciliates
    Night's portents with holy spelt and a dance of salt.   10
Yet, however it be, whether they wish truly to be warned
    Or wish to put their trust in the lies of sleep,
May Lucina make delusive the terrors of the night and wish
    That the dread felt by the innocent be only vain,
If neither my mind is answerable for an ugly deed   15
    Nor my wicked tongue has vexed the mighty gods.
Nox in her black team's chariot had already traversed the sky
    Of heaven and bathed its wheels in Ocean's blue,
And the god who succors an anxious mind had brought me no rest:
    Somnus falters before the homes of the distressed.   20
At last, when Phoebus looked out from the peak of his rising,
    Tardy sleep weighed down my enfeebled eyes.
Then a youth, his temples crowned with holy laurel,
    Seemed to set his foot within our abode.

Non vidit quicquam formosius ulla priorum 25
Aetas, humanum nec fuit illud opus.
Intonsi crines longa cervice fluebant,
Stillabat Syrio myrtea rore coma.
Candor erat qualem praefert Latonia Luna,
Et color in niveo corpore purpureus, 30
Ut iuveni primum virgo deducta marito
Inficitur teneras ore rubente genas,
Et cum contexunt amarantis alba puellae
Lilia et autumno candida mala rubent.
Ima videbatur talis illudere palla: 35
Namque haec in nitido corpore vestis erat.
Artis opus rarae, fulgens testudine et auro
Pendebat laeva garrula parte lyra.
Hanc primum veniens plectro modulatus eburno
Felices cantus ore sonante dedit. 40
Sed postquam fuerant digiti cum voce locuti,
Edidit haec dulci tristia verba modo:
'Salue, cura deum: casto nam rite poetae
Phoebusque et Bacchus Pieridesque favent,
Sed proles Semelae Bacchus doctaeque sorores 45
Dicere non norunt, quid ferat hora sequens.
At mihi fatorum leges aevique futuri
Eventura pater posse videre dedit.
Quare, ego quae dico non fallax, accipe, vates
Quodque deus vero Cynthius ore feram. 50
Tantum cara tibi, quantum nec filia matri,
Quantum nec cupido bella puella viro,
Pro qua sollicitas caelestia numina votis,
Quae tibi securos non sinit ire dies
Et, cum te fusco Somnus velavit amictu, 55
Vanum nocturnis fallit imaginibus,
Carminibus celebrata tuis formosa Neaera
Alterius mavult esse puella viri,
Diversasque tuis agitat mens impia curas,
Nec gaudet casta nupta Neaera domo. 60

4.34: *et* for *ut*.
4.39: *veniens* for *feriens*.

No era of our ancestors saw anything more handsome. 25
 He was not the creation of humankind.
His unshorn hair streamed the length of his graceful neck;
 His locks dripped with the myrrh of Syrian dew.
His brilliance was such as Latona's Luna displays,
 And crimson the shimmer on his snow-bright limbs, 30
As a maiden, first escorted to her young husband,
 Blushes, her tender cheeks stained with red,
Or when girls entwine white lilies with amaranths,
 And bright apples redden at autumn time.
His mantle's hem seemed to frolic around his ankles: 35
 For this was the garment that clothed his gleaming limbs.
On his left side hung his loquacious lyre, rare skill's
 Creation, gleaming with tortoiseshell and gold.
As he entered he first strummed it with ivory quill,
 And uttered cheering song from his resonant lips. 40
But after fingers and voice had spoken together,
 These sad words he pronounced in limpid tones:
"Hail, ward of the gods, for Phoebus, Bacchus, and the Pierides
 Duly cherish the poet's nobility.
But Bacchus, Semele's child, and the learnèd sisters 45
 Have not mastered what the next hour brings.
My father, though, has allotted me the power to divine
 The laws of the Fates and the outcome of future time.
So give ear, O poet, to what I, an undeceiving seer, have to say,
 To what I express, Cynthus's truthful god. 50
She who is as dear to you as no daughter ever was to mother,
 As no graceful girl ever was to her yearning spouse,
On whose behalf you pester the powers of heaven with prayers,
 Who never allows your days to pass without worry
And, when Somnus has clothed you in his dusky robe, 55
 Deceives you, fool, with specters in the night,
Neaera the beautiful, extolled through your songs,
 Prefers to be the girl of another man.
Her wicked heart busies itself with concerns not your own.
 No joys are Neaera's as wife in a holy home. 60

A crudele genus nec fidum femina nomen!
    A pereat, didicit fallere siqua virum!
Sed flecti poterit (mens est mutabilis illis):
    Tu modo cum multa bracchia tende prece.
Saevus Amor docuit validos temptare labores,   65
    Saevus Amor docuit verbera posse pati.
Me quondam Admeti niveas pavisse iuvencas
    Non est in vanum fabula ficta iocum:
Tunc ego nec cithara poteram gaudere sonora
    Nec similes chordis reddere voce sonos,   70
Sed perlucenti cantum meditabar avena
    Ille ego Latonae filius atque Iovis.
Nescis quid sit amor, iuvenis, si ferre recusas
    Immitem dominam coniugiumque ferum.
Ergo ne dubita blandas adhibere querelas: 75
    Vincuntur molli pectora dura prece.
Quod si vera canunt sacris oracula templis,
    Haec illi nostro nomine dicta refer:
Hoc tibi coniugium promittit Delius ipse:
    Felix hoc alium desine velle virum.'   80
Dixit et ignavus defluxit corpore somnus.
    A ego ne possim tanta videre mala!
Nec tibi crediderim votis contraria vota
    Nec tantum crimen pectore inesse tuo:
Nam te nec vasti genuerunt aequora ponti   85
    Nec flammam volvens ore Chimaera fero
Nec canis anguina redimitus terga caterva,
    Cui tres sunt linguae tergeminumque caput,
Scyllaque virgineam canibus succincta figuram,
    Nec te conceptam saeva leaena tulit,   90
Barbara nec Scythiae tellus horrendave Syrtis,
    Sed culta et duris non habitanda domus
Et longe ante alias omnes mitissima mater
    Isque pater quo non alter amabilior.
Haec deus in melius crudelia somnia vertat   95
    Et iubeat tepidos irrita ferre Notos.

Oh, cruel breed! Oh, faithless race of womankind!
    Death to her who has learned to deceive her man!
But she can be guided. Their minds are fickle. Do you
    Only stretch forth your arms to her with many a prayer.
Fierce Amor taught how to brave intense trials,   65
    Fierce Amor taught to endure the lash.
It is no myth, coined for a foolish laugh, that once upon a time
    I fed the snow-bright heifers of Admetus.
At that time I could take no joy in the cithara's song
    Nor with my voice sing back in kind to its strings,   70
But on light-filled reed I rehearsed my song—
    I, the son of Latona and of Jove!
Young man, you are ignorant of love, if you do not abide
    A ruthless mistress and a cruel union.
So do not hesitate to apply the flattery of lament: 75
    Hard hearts are won by the gentleness of prayer.
But if from holy temples oracles sing the truth,
    Then forward to her these words under my name:
The Delian himself promises to you this marriage.
    Happy with him, cease to yearn for another man."   80
He spoke, and slothful sleep slipped away from my limbs.
    Ah, may I not cast eyes on such great evil!
I could not believe that your vows were the opposite of mine,
    Nor that such a crime lurked within your breast.
For the waters of the dreary sea did not beget you,   85
    Nor the Chimaera, rolling fire from its savage mouth,
Nor the dog with a back encircled by a throng of snakes,
    Possessed of triple tongues and a triple head,
Nor Scylla, her virgin's frame girdled with dogs; nor were you
    Conceived and borne by a savage lioness,   90
Nor by Scythia's barbarous terrain, nor the dread Syrtis,
    But a refined dwelling, no refuge for the harsh,
And far beyond all others the gentlest of mothers,
    And a father more lovable than any other.
May the god turn this cruel dream to the better, and ordain   95
    The warm Noti to bear it off as vain.

5

Vos tenet, Etruscis manat quae fontibus unda,
  Unda sub aestivum non adeunda Canem,
Nunc autem sacris Baiarum proxima lymphis,
  Cum se purpureo vere remittit humus:
At mihi Persephone nigram denuntiat horam: 5
  Immerito iuveni parce nocere, dea.
Non ego temptavi nulli temeranda virorum
  Audax laudandae sacra docere deae,
Nec mea mortiferis infecit pocula sucis
  Dextera nec cuiquam trita venena dedit,   10
Nec nos sacrilegi templis amovimus ignes,
  Nec cor sollicitant facta nefanda meum,
Nec nos insana meditantes iurgia mente
  Impia in aversos solvimus ora deos:
Et nondum cani nigros laesere capillos,   15
  Nec venit tardo curva senecta pede:
Natalem primo nostrum videre parentes,
  Cum cecidit fato consul uterque pari.
Quid fraudare iuvat vitem crescentibus uvis
  Et modo nata mala vellere poma manu?   20
Parcite, pallentes undas quicumque tenetis
  Duraque sortiti tertia regna dei.
Elysios olim liceat cognoscere campos
  Lethaeamque ratem Cimmeriosque lacus,
Cum mea rugosa pallebunt ora senecta   25
  Et referam pueris tempora prisca senex.
Atque utinam vano nequiquam terrear aestu!
  Languent ter quinos sed mea membra dies.
At vobis Tuscae celebrantur numina lymphae
  Et facilis lenta pellitur unda manu.   30
Vivite felices, memores et vivite nostri,
  Sive erimus seu nos fata fuisse volent.
Interea nigras pecudes promittite Diti
  Et nivei lactis pocula mixta mero.

5.10: *trita* for *taetra*.
5.27: *terrear* for *torrear*.

5. The Poet's Concern

The stream holds you fast that flows from Etruscan springs, stream
    Not to be approached in Canis's summertime,
But now quite akin to the revered waters of Baiae,
    When the ground relaxes during purpled spring.
Yet Persephone threatens me with a time of blackness.   5
    O Goddess, harm not an undeserving youth!
I have not rashly sought to teach the revered goddess's
    Rites, not to be sullied by men's presence.
My hand has not tainted goblets with juices meant to kill,
    Nor offered poisons crushed for someone's ruin,   10
Nor in any sinfulness have I set fire to temples
    Nor do evil misdeeds harass my heart,
Nor, pondering curses in my maddened mind, have I
    Directed impious words toward hostile gods.
And not yet has white tainted my dark locks,   15
    Nor has bent old age arrived on shuffling foot.
My parents first beheld my hour of birth the day
    When each consul fell by one and the same fate.
What gain to cheat a vine of its ripening grapes
    Or with heinous hand pluck the newborn fruit!   20
Spare me, O you gods who govern the sallow waters
    And the merciless realms you gained in third place.
Only one day may I come to know Elysium's fields,
    The boat of Lethe and Cimmerian pools,
When my face is sallow from the wrinkles of old age   25
    And in old age I will report times past to the young.
If only my fears of a trifling fever were in vain!
    But for thrice five days my limbs have felt unwell.
Yet the Naiads of Tuscan waters are thronged by you
    And the easy wave parted with unhurried hand.   30
Prosper and be mindful of us, whether
    We live on or Fate wishes our time has come.
Meanwhile make promise of black sheep to Dis
    And goblets of snow-bright milk infused with wine.

6

Candide Liber, ades (sic sit tibi mystica vitis
    Semper, sic hedera tempora vincta geras),
Aufer et ipse meum, patera medicante, dolorem:
    Saepe tuo cecidit munere victus amor.
Care puer, madeant generoso pocula Baccho,   5
    Et nobis prona funde Falerna manu.
Ite procul, durum curae genus, ite labores:
    Fulserit hic niveis Delius alitibus.
Vos modo proposito dulces faveatis amici
    Neve neget quisquam me duce se comitem,   10
Aut, si quis vini certamen mite recusat,
    Fallat eum tecto cara puella dolo.
Ille facit mites animos deus, ille ferocem
    Contundit et dominae misit in arbitrium,
Armeniasque tigres et fulvas ille leaenas   15
    Vicit et indomitis mollia corda dedit.
Haec Amor et maiora valet. Sed poscite Bacchi
    Munera: quem vestrum pocula sicca iuvant?
Convenit ex aequo nec torvus Liber in illos
    Qui se quique una vina iocosa colunt: 20
At venit iratus nimium nimiumque severis:
    Qui timet irati numina magna, bibat.
Quales his poenas deus hic quantasque minetur,
    Cadmeae matris praeda cruenta docet.
Sed procul a nobis hic sit timor, illaque, siqua est   25
    Quid valeat laesi sentiat ira dei.
Quid precor a demens? Venti temeraria vota,
    Aeriae et nubes diripienda ferant.
Quamvis nulla mei superest tibi cura, Neaera,
    Sis felix et sint candida fata tua.   30
At nos securae reddamus tempora mensae:
    Venit post nimbos una serena dies.
Ei mihi, difficile est imitari gaudia falsa,
    Difficile est tristi fingere mente iocum,

6.3: *aufer* for *affer*; *meum* for *merum*; *patera medicante* for *Pater, et medicare.*
6.13: *mites* for *dites.*

6. A Prayer to Bacchus

Bright Liber, come near—so may the mystic vine be ever yours;
    So may you ever display brows bound with ivy—
Yourself take away my suffering with the cup that cures.
    Love, conquered by your gift, has often fallen.
Dear lad, may your goblets be steeped in noble Bacchus,   5
    Pour the Falernian for us with tilted hand.
Away afar, harsh race of sorrow; away, troubles:
    Here the Delian should shine with his snow-bright birds.
Only, sweet friends, please approve what I have proposed
    Nor let anyone fail to ally himself to my lead.   10
Or if anyone say no to a gentle bout with wine
    May his dear girl trick him with deceit well hid.
That god calms our spirits. He has crushed the savage
    And sent him under his mistress's command,
And has subdued tigers of Armenia and tawny lionesses   15
    And has bestowed gentle hearts on the untamed.
Amor has these powers, and greater still. Demand Bacchus's gifts!
    Do sober drafts please any one of you?
Not grim but as compeer Liber greets those
    Who together worship him, worship happy wine.   20
But angry, very angry is his approach to the austere.
    Who fears the great god's anger, let him drink.
With what enormous reprisal this god threatens them
    The bloodied quarry of the Cadmean mother warns.
But far from us be this fear. Let her, if such a one exist,   25
    Experience the powerful rage of an affronted god.
What madness is my prayer! May the winds and the lofty clouds .
    Carry off and dissolve the rashness of my vows.
Neaera, though no concern for me remains yours,
    Be happy! And may your destiny be bright!   30
But let us ourselves devote time to carefree banqueting:
    After the rains an unclouded day has come.
Alas for me, hard it is to counterfeit feigned joys,
    Hard to fake delight with an embittered heart.

Nec bene mendaci risus componitur ore,   35
   Nec bene sollicitis ebria verba sonant.
Quid queror infelix? Turpes discedite curae:
   Odit Lenaeus tristia verba pater.
Cnosia, Theseae quondam periuria linguae
   Flevisti ignoto sola relicta mari: 40
Sic cecinit pro te doctus, Minoi, Catullus
   Ingrati referens impia facta viri.
Vos ego nunc moneo: felix, quicumque dolore
   Alterius disces posse cavere tuum.
Nec vos aut capiant pendentia bracchia collo   45
   Aut fallat blanda subdola lingua prece.
Etsi perque suos fallax iurabit ocellos
   Iunonemque suam perque suam Venerem,
Nulla fides inerit: periuria ridet amantum
   Iuppiter et ventos irrita ferre iubet.   50
Ergo quid totiens fallacis verba puellae
   Conqueror? Ite a me, seria verba, precor.
Quam vellem tecum longas requiescere noctes
   Et tecum longos pervigilare dies,
Perfida nec merito nobis nec amica merenti,   55
   Perfida, sed, quamvis perfida, cara tamen!
Naida Bacchus amat: cessas, o lente minister?
   Temperet annosum Marcia lympha merum.
Non ego, si fugiat nostrae convivia mensae
   Ignotum cupiens vana puella torum,   60
Sollicitus repetam tota suspiria nocte.
   I, puer, et liquidum fortius adde merum.
Iam dudum Syrio madefactus tempora nardo
   Debueram sertis implicuisse comas.

6.44: *tuum* for *tuo.*
6.52: *precor* for *procul.*

A smile is not aptly concocted on a lying face,   35
    Not aptly ring tipsy words from anxious lips.
Wretched, why do I complain? Depart, ugly worries!
    Father Lenaeus abhors bitter words.
Once, girl of Cnossos, you wept for the lies from Theseus's tongue,
    Abandoned, alone, on an unfamiliar sea.   40
Thus for you, daughter of Minos, learnèd Catullus sang,
    Recounting the evil deeds of your thankless spouse.
So I now give you warning: happy you who learn
    From another's grief to be able to avoid your own.
Do not let arms, dangling around your neck, control you,   45
    Nor treacherous tongue deceive with flattering plea.
Though the deceiver will swear by her very eyes,
    By Juno herself, by Venus's very self,
There will be nothing to trust. Jupiter laughs at lovers' lies,
    And orders winds to carry them off as vain.   50
So why do I so often lament my deceitful girl's words?
    Away from me, I pray, any words of weight!
How could I yearn to rest long nights with you,
    To pass the long days' waking hours with you,
Faithless to the undeserved, unloving to the deserved,   55
    Faithless to us, though nonetheless dear?
Bacchus loves a Naiad. Why hang back, slave slow to pour?
    Let Marcia's water tame our ancient wine.
If a fickle girl, yearning for a stranger's bed, flees
    The entertainment of our board, I will not   60
Worry the whole night through with constant sighs. Come, boy!
    And boldly, boldly add the clear pure wine.
Long since, my brows dripping with the nard of Syria,
    I ought to have twined some garlands in my hair.

Sulpicia

Corpus Tibullianum: Liber Tertius, 13–18

1 (3.13)

Tandem venit amor, qualem texisse pudori
    Quam nudasse alicui sit mihi fama magis.
Exorata meis illum Cytherea Camenis
    Attulit in nostrum deposuitque sinum.
Exsolvit promissa Venus: mea gaudia narret,   5
    Dicetur siquis non habuisse sua.
Non ego signatis quicquam mandare tabellis,
    Me legat ut nemo quam meus ante, velim,
Sed peccasse iuvat, vultus componere famae
    Taedet: cum digno digna fuisse ferar.   10

2 (3.14)

Invisus natalis adest, qui rure molesto
    Et sine Cerintho tristis agendus erit.
Dulcius urbe quid est? An villa sit apta puellae
    Atque Arretino frigidus amnis agro?
Iam, nimium Messalla mei studiose, quiescas: 5
    Non tempestivae saepe, propinque, viae.
Hic animum sensusque meos abducta relinquo
    Arbitrio quam uis non sinit esse meo.

1.6: *sua* for *suam*.
1.8: *me legat ut nemo* for *ne legat id nemo*.
2.4: *amnis* for *Arnus*.
2.6: *non* for *neu*.
2.8: *arbitrio* for *arbitrii*; *sinit* for *satis*; *meo* for *mei*.

Sulpicia

Corpus Tibullianum 3.13–18 = 4.7–12

1. The Poet's Love

At last a love has come such that repute of having hid it
　　Would shame me more than had I laid it bare.
Persuaded by my Camenae the Cytherean has guided him
　　Toward me, and lodged him in my lap.
Venus discharged her promise. Let anyone tell of my joys　　　　5
　　If he will be said to have lacked his own.
I would not wish to entrust my words to tablets under seal
　　That none may read me before my love.
To stray is my pleasure. To feign for reputation's sake I am loath.
　　Worthy I will be said, and to consort with worth.　　　　10

2. A Birthday Away

My hated birthday is come, to be passed in sorrow and vexation
　　Off in the country—and without my Cerinthus.
What is sweeter than the city? Is a manor house suited to a girl
　　And a chill brook in provincial Arretium?
Rest now at ease, Messalla, overeager for my welfare:　　　　5
　　Journeys, my kinsman, are often inopportune.
Though far away, here I leave my feelings and my soul,
　　Whom force does not allow to be under my own control.

3 (3.15)

Scis iter ex animo sublatum triste puellae?
    Natali Romae iam licet esse meo.
Omnibus ille dies nobis natalis agatur,
    Qui nec opinanti nunc tibi forte venit.

4 (3.16)

Gratum est, securus multum quod iam tibi de me
    Permittis, subito ne male inepta cadam.
Sit tibi cura togae potior pressumque quasillo
    Scortum quam Servi filia Sulpicia:
Solliciti sunt pro nobis, quibus illa doloris   5
    Ne cedam ignoto maxima causa toro.

5 (3.17)

Estne tibi, Cerinthe, tuae pia cura puellae,
    Quod mea nunc vexat corpora fessa calor?
A ego non aliter tristes evincere morbos
    Optarim, quam te si quoque velle putem.
At mihi quid prosit morbos evincere, si tu   5
    Nostra potes lento pectore ferre mala?

6 (3.18)

Ne tibi sim, mea lux, aeque iam fervida cura,
    Ac videor paucos ante fuisse dies,
Si quicquam tota commisi stulta iuventa
    Cuius me fatear paenituisse magis,
Hesterna quam te solum quod nocte reliqui,   5
    Ardorem cupiens dissimulare meum.

3.2: *meo* for *tuo.*
3.4: *opinanti . . . forte* for *opinata . . . sorte.*
4.2: *permittis* for *promittis.*
4.3: *sit* for *si.*

3. Birthday in Rome

Do you know that the sad journey is lifted from your girl's mind?
    I am allowed to spend my birthday now at Rome.
Let that day of birth be enjoyed by all of us,
    Which of a sudden arrives for you now by chance.

4. A Rebuke to Cerinthus

I thank you that, in your assurance, you grant yourself great leeway
    About me, lest quite the fool I suddenly tumble!
The toga and a whore, weighted with wool's creel, may be your
    Greater concern than Servius's daughter, Sulpicia.
They are worried on our behalf whose greatest reason for disgust   5
    Is lest I yield my place to a lowborn lust.

5. The Ill Poet to Her Lover

Cerinthus, have you no loyal concern for your girl,
    When fever now torments my weakened frame?
Ah, I would not yearn to overcome the grim disease
    Unless I thought you wished the very same.
What good for me to overcome disease, if you   5
    Can bear my woes with apathetic soul?

6. The Poet's Apology

My light, let me not be to you now so blazing a passion
    As I seem to have been just a few days in the past,
If in all my youth I foolishly have achieved something
    Of which I might admit I have repented more
Than that last night I left you all alone   5
    In my desire to mask my burning flame.

Domitii Marsi

Te quoque Vergilio comitem non aequa, Tibulle,
    Mors iuvenem campos misit ad Elysios
ne foret aut elegis molles qui fleret amores
    aut caneret forti regia bella pede.

Domitius Marsus

On the Death of Tibullus

You were still a young man, Tibullus, but unjust Mors
    Sent you to the Elysian Fields as Virgil's companion,
That none should be left to weep soft loves in elegies
    Or to sing battles of kings in powerful measures.

Ovid *Amores* 3.9

Memnona si mater, mater ploravit Achillem,
    et tangunt magnas tristia fata deas,
flebilis indignos, Elegia, solve capillos:
    a, nimis ex vero nunc tibi nomen erit!
ille tui vates operis, tua fama, Tibullus   5
    ardet in exstructo, corpus inane, rogo.
ecce puer Veneris fert eversamque pharetram
    et fractos arcus et sine luce facem;
adspice, demissis ut eat miserabilis alis
    pectoraque infesta tundat aperta manu.   10
excipiunt lacrimas sparsi per colla capilli,
    oraque singultu concutiente sonant.
fratris in Aeneae sic illum funere dicunt
    egressum tectis, pulcher Iule, tuis;
nec minus est confusa Venus moriente Tibullo,   15
    quam iuveni rupit cum ferus inguen aper.
at sacri vates et divum cura vocamur,
    sunt etiam qui nos numen habere putent.
scilicet omne sacrum Mors importuna profanat,
    omnibus obscuras inicit illa manus.   20
quid pater Ismario, quid mater, profuit Orpheo,
    carmine quid victas obstipuisse feras?
et Linon in silvis idem pater 'aelinon' altis
    dicitur invita concinuisse lyra.
adice Maeoniden, a quo ceu fonte perenni   25
    vatum Pieriis ora rigantur aquis;
hunc quoque summa dies nigro summersit Averno:
    defugiunt avidos carmina sola rogos.

durat opus vatum, Troiani fama laboris
 tardaque nocturno tela retexta dolo: 30
sic Nemesis longum, sic Delia nomen habebunt,
 altera cura recens, altera primus amor.
Quid vos sacra iuvant? quid nunc Aegyptia prosunt
 sistra? quid in vacuo secubuisse toro?
cum rapiunt mala fata bonos, (ignoscite fasso)   35
 sollicitor nullos esse putare deos.
vive pius: moriere; pius cole sacra: colentem
 Mors gravis a templis in cava busta trahet;
carminibus confide bonis: iacet ecce Tibullus:
 vix manet e toto, parva quod urna capit.   40
tene, sacer vates, flammae rapuere rogales
 pectoribus pasci nec timuere tuis?
aurea sanctorum potuissent templa deorum
 urere, quae tantum sustinuere nefas.
avertit vultus, Erycis quae possidet arces;   45
 sunt quoque qui lacrimas continuisse negant.
sed tamen hoc melius, quam si Phaeacia tellus
 ignotum vili supposuisset humo.
hic certe madidos fugientis pressit ocellos
 mater et in cineres ultima dona tulit;   50
hic soror in partem misera cum matre doloris
 venit inornatas dilaniata comas,
cumque tuis sua iunxerunt Nemesisque priorque
 oscula nec solos destituere rogos.
Delia discendens 'felicius' inquit 'amata   55
 sum tibi; vixisti, dum tuus ignis eram.'
cui Nemesis 'quid' ait 'tibi sunt mea damna dolori?
 me tenuit moriens deficiente manu.'
si tamen e nobis aliquid nisi nomen et umbra
 restat, in Elysia valle Tibullus erit.   60
obvius huic venies hedera iuvenalia cinctus
 tempora cum Calvo, docte Catulle, tuo;
tu quoque, si falsum est temerati crimen amici,
 sanguinis atque animae prodige Galle tuae.
his comes umbra tua est; si qua est modo corporis umbra;   65
 auxisti numeros, culte Tibulle, pios.
ossa quieta, precor, tuta requiescite in urna,
 et sit humus cineri non onerosa tuo.

If his mother had mourned Memnon, if his mother had mourned Achilles, and if sad fates touch great goddesses, loose your undeserving locks, doleful Elegy! Yes, your name now will be all too truthful! He, your art's poet, your glory, Tibullus, burns, an empty body on the lofty pyre. Watch: the child of Venus carries his quiver reversed and broken bows and a torch without light; look how sadly he comes, wings drooping, and how he beats his bared chest with savage hand. [10] His locks, scattered about his neck, catch his tears, and his lips sound with the shaking of sobs. So they say he behaved at the funeral of his brother, Aeneas, when he came forth from your home, beautiful Iulus. Nor was Venus less troubled at the death of Tibullus than when the ferocious boar crushed the groin of her young man.

We poets are indeed called sacred and the care of the gods; there are even those who think we have divine power. Yet it is certain that demanding Mors profanes everything sacred; she lays her darkening hands on everything. [20] What help was his father to Ismarian Orpheus, what help his mother, what help that the wild beasts he had mastered were dumbstruck by his song? The same sire is said to have mourned Linus—*Woe, Linus!*— in the woods on unwilling lyre. Add the Maeonian bard, from whom as from an ever-flowing fountain the lips of poets are watered from the Pierian spring; him also the final day submerged in black Avernus: songs alone escape greedy pyres. The work of poets lasts, the renown of the struggle at Troy and the slow web unwoven by deceit at night. [30] So Nemesis, so Delia will possess lasting repute: the one his recent amour; the other his first love.

What aid were your rites? What help now your Egyptian rattles? What your sleeping apart on an empty bed? When evil fates snatch away the good—Forgive my declaration!—I am tempted to think that no gods exist! Live in a holy manner; you will die. Perform rites in holy fashion: as you worship, heavy Mors will drag you from temple to hollow grave. Trust in the beauty of song: see, Tibullus lies dead; from his whole body scarcely remains what a tiny urn receives. [40] Have the flames of the pyre snatched you away, blessed poet, and have they had no fear to gnaw at your breast? Flames that supported so great a crime could have burned the golden temples of the holy gods. She who controls the citadel of Eryx turned her glance away; there are also those who say that she failed to hold back tears.

Nevertheless this is better than if the land of Phaeacia had buried you, unknown, in its beggarly earth. Here as you fled away your mother closed your brimming eyes and gave the final gifts to your ashes. [50] Here your sister, her disheveled locks torn, came to share your sorrowing mother's grief, and Nemesis and her predecessor joined their kisses with your kin's and did not abandon your pyre to itself. Withdrawing from it Delia says: "More happily was I loved by you. You remained alive as long as you were my flame." Nemesis replies: "Why are you mourning for my loss? As he died I was the one that he held with failing hand."

Yet, if any part of us survives except name and shade, Tibullus will find a place in the Valley of Elysium. [60] Learnèd Catullus, you will come to greet him, your youthful temples circled with ivy, together with your Calvus; you also, Gallus, lavish with your blood and your soul, if the charge that you betrayed your friend is untrue. Your shade is their comrade, if there is any shade when the body is gone; you, refined Tibullus, have added to the number of the blessèd. I pray: O bones, repose quietly in the quietude of your safe urn, and may no heavy weight of earth rest on your ash.

Notes to the Translations

TIBULLUS, BOOK I

1.11–12   The reference is probably to Terminus, Roman god of boundaries. For further detail, see commentators on Livy 1.55.4–5; Ovid *Fasti* 2.639–84.

1.14   Tibullus is referring to Silvanus, Roman god of agriculture. See commentators on Virgil *Eclogue* 10.24, *Aeneid* 8.601.

1.17   Priapus was a fertility god with a prominent phallus, respected in particular as protector of gardens. Statues of the god were often painted red, especially for holidays. He is also the subject of a poem by Horace (*Satires* 1.8) and of a collection of *Priapea*.

1.19–22   A probable reference to losses incurred as the result of Rome's many years of civil war.

1.27   The rising of Sirius, the Dog Star in the constellation Canis Major, a few days after the summer solstice, ushered in the hottest season of the year.

1.36   Pales, tutelary divinity of herds and flocks, was celebrated at the Parilia on April 21, the traditional date for the foundation of Rome.

1.54   Spoils taken from a conquered enemy were often displayed in the *vestibulum* of the victorious hero's house.

1.56   An anticipation of the subsequent poem's theme, the mistress's unresponsive house-door.

1.67   The Roman Manes, from Old Latin *manus, manuus* ("good"), were the deified spirits of the dead.

2   The poem is a form of *paraklausithyron*, words purportedly sung before the closed door of a mistress. Its theme is varied as well by Catullus, Propertius, Ovid, and their imitators.

2.16   An elegist's variation on the adage "Fortes Fortuna adiuvat" ("Fortune abets the brave"), first found in Terence (*Phormio* 203).

2.28   In early Latin a robber who stole cloaks at night was called a *praemiator* ("a 'reward' collector").

2.29–30   As both lover and, implicitly, poet, the speaker is doubly sacrosanct.

2.35   To behold what one shouldn't could well bring on a curse.

2.41–42   Venus-Aphrodite grew from the "foam" created when Cronus threw the genitals of his father, Uranus, whom he had castrated, into the sea near the island of Cythera.

2.45–54   Standard capabilities for witches, according to the Roman poets. See, e.g., commentators on Virgil *Eclogue* 8.69–71.

2.56   Spitting was supposed by the ancients, as it is in many more recent societies, to have an apotropaic effect. See below, 2.98, and Pliny the Elder *Historia naturalis* 28.35–39.

2.64   A drab-colored offering would be appropriate for the divinities of a shadowy world.

2.80   We are meant to imagine ourselves within a Roman house, listening to a fountain playing at the center of its peristyle.

2.96   Though the Forum of Caesar had been dedicated in 46 B.C.E., the Forum Romanum, the chief public square and business center of ancient Rome, is probably meant.

3.1   Marcus Valerius Messalla Corvinus (64 B.C.E.–8 C.E.), Roman orator, soldier, and statesman, was Tibullus's patron as well as uncle of the poet Sulpicia. For his military campaigns after the battle of Actium, see on the opening lines of Tibullus 1.7.

3.11   Divination by sortilege was a common practice in antiquity.

3.14   To stare in such a situation would be an act of ill omen.

3.18   Saturn's day, modern Saturday, would be the seventh day of the planetary week, the Jewish Sabbath. The god's reign is regularly connected with the Golden Age, some characteristics of which Tibullus details at lines 35–48.

3.27–28   Paintings affixed to the goddess's temple walls were votive offerings acknowledging her help in effecting cures.

3.37   Tibullus is implicitly referring to the *Argo* and its famous originating journey.

3.49   We are now in the Iron Age of the tyrannical reign of Jupiter, who overpowered his father, Saturn.

3.55–56   The Roman elegists are fond of weaving epitaphs into their poems, especially as conclusions. Cf. also, for instance, Lygdamus 2.29–30. For a detailed discussion, see Ramsby.

3.66   The plant myrtle was sacred to Venus.

3.67   Greek Tartarus, pagan equivalent of the Christian hell.

4.21–22   The commonplace that the lies of lovers remain unpunished goes back to Catullus 30.10 and 64.59 and 142, probable sources of Tibullus's language here.

4.23–24   Jupiter lied to Juno about his liaison with Io.

4.38   As early as Homer (*Iliad* 20.39; see also *Homeric Hymn* 3 [*To Delian Apollo*] 134), Apollo is described as having unshorn hair. For Dionysus's dark hair that waves around him, see *Homeric Hymn* 7.4–5.

4.40   Tibullus is thinking of Virgil's aphoristic "Love conquers all" ("omnia vincit Amor," *Eclogue* 10.69).

4.49–50   To carry the nets would be a slave's task.

4.59–60   Cursing an inventor is a commonplace found in classical literature as early as Euripides (*Hippolytus* 407–9). See also 1.10.1–2.

4.67–70   The poet curses the venal boy with the wish that he become one of the maddened Galli, eunuch followers of Cybele, the Magna Mater. The tale of a particular Gallus is the subject of Catullus 63.

5.3   The simile has much in common with Virgil's at *Aeneid* 7.378–83, where Amata roused by the Fury Allecto is compared to a top set spinning.

5.4   The "swift boy" is Cupid.

5.14   Salted grain ("mola salsa") was utilized in a variety of sacrificial rites. See commentators on Horace *Satires* 2.3.200.

5.24   Must is the unfermented, or partly fermented, grape juice for making wine.

5.27   Probably Silvanus is meant.

5.45–46   Thetis, daughter of the sea god Nereus, was courted by Peleus after she rode to the Thessalian shore on her dolphin. The story is told in greater detail by Ovid (*Metamorphoses* 11.229–65).

5.65–66   It was Roman custom to remove sandals before dinner. Maltby's note *ad locum* is excellent: "The first meaning is that the poor man would escort his mistress to her friends' dinner parties.... Again a *double entendre* seems likely. The poor man will escort his mistress to secret assignations with her lovers."

6.24   Blindness would be a possible punishment for the profanation of a divinity, in this case if a man attended a ceremony meant only for women.

6.39–40   Signs of suspect masculinity.

6.45   Bellona, Roman personification of war. With her bloody whip she makes a dramatic appearance at Virgil *Aeneid* 8.703.

6.67–68   The hair fillet and long gown (*stola*) were distinctive and, in the latter case, exclusive attributes of a Roman matron's dress from as early as the third century B.C.E.

7.1   According to Catullus (64.306–22), the Fates sang as they spun out human destiny.

7.3–12   Messalla's operations in Gaul would have taken place in what is roughly the southwest of modern France.

7.17   White doves were sacred to Syro-Phoenician Astarte.

7.19–20   Though the ancients more readily credited the invention of sailing to the Egyptians, the Phoenicians were also well known as seafarers and merchantmen.

7.23–24   The source of the Nile was unknown in antiquity and not discovered until the ninteenth century. For this reason his statue is represented with head veiled in Bernini's splendid Fountain of the Four Rivers, finished in 1651, at the center of the Piazza Navona in Rome.

7.39   Osiris was identified with Bacchus-Dionysus by the Greeks. (See Herodotus *History* 2.42.)

7.48 A wickerwork basket contained mystic objects associated with the rites of the god.

7.49 His Genius is a man's spirit, born to him at birth and hence worshipped appropriately on a birthday. He is often depicted as a togaed statue that forms part of a household's shrine to its Lares.

7.57–58 At the end of the Roman civil wars Messalla was authorized to repair part of the Via Latina, which leaves Rome toward the southeast and crosses the Alban Hills between Tusculum and Alba Longa. Tibullus therefore imagines someone detained east of Rome and thinking of his way back to the city. "Bright" (Latin *candida*) puns on the meaning of *alba* ("white").

8.3–4 Tibullus alludes to three forms of divination: sortilege, haruspicy (scrutiny of entrails), and augury (observation of birds). For the first, see also Tibullus 1.3.11–12.

8.5–6 The lover learns from his servitude to Venus.

8.19 As early as the Twelve Tables (traditionally dated to 451/0 B.C.E.) punishment was given to someone who "charmed crops" from one place to another. See Virgil *Eclogue* 8.99; Pliny the Elder *Historia naturalis* 28.18.

8.20 Cf., e.g., Virgil *Eclogue* 8.71.

8.21–22 The clashing of bronze instruments was supposed to frighten whoever was responsible for the moon's eclipse. See Virgil *Eclogue* 8.69.

8.44 A reference to the walnut's outer bark.

9.24 Perhaps Amor or Cupido is meant.

9.42 This was the task of a slave.

10.10 Varro (*Res rusticae* 2.2.4) makes it clear that sheep with speckled fleece were unwelcome in a flock. But perhaps our poet, in a less practical vein, may be suggesting a remembrance of Virgil's *Eclogue* 4, where variegated sheep are the mark of a golden age.

10.36 The sailor is Charon, who ferried souls across the Styx.

10.48 The handing down of property from father to son is a commonplace in the Roman writers. See, e.g., Virgil *Eclogue* 9.50.

TIBULLUS, BOOK 2

1 The poem as a whole documents a festival that purifies the fields, probably the Ambarvalia, celebrated on May 29.

1.11–13 Such instructions demanding celibacy are common (cf. also Tibullus 1.3.25–26) as is the commanding away of any offenders against such rules.

1.27 Romans dated their wines by the consul of the vintage's year. Wine casks, both exterior and interior, were smoked in a *fumarium*. (See Columella *De re rustica* 1.6.19.) The smoke was believed to help mature the wine.

1.34 According to Varro (*Res rusticae,* 2.11.10) and Pliny the Elder (*Historia naturalis* 7.211), shaving became usual for the Romans beginning in 300 B.C.E.

1.49 According to some ancient authorities, bees carried flowers.

1.53   Tibullus is drawing on Virgil *Eclogue* 10.51. See also below on Lygdamus 4.71.

1.55   As part of the celebration the farmer painted himself red with cinnabar, as did Roman generals at their triumphs (Pliny the Elder *Historia naturalis* 33.111).

1.66   An alternative reading has *later* ("brick") instead of *latus* ("side"), as translated here. If the former is correct, Tibullus is referring to the brick weights that held the warp taut.

1.68   A reference to *hippomanes* ("horse-madness"), a secretion from mares in heat used in love philters. Cf. also Virgil *Georgics* 3.266–83.

2.18   The Romans associated the color yellow with marriage. (See commentators on Catullus 61.8–10.)

3.14b   After the lacuna we are learning how to make whey.

3.17   Diana is meant.

3.24   The reference is to Juno, actually Apollo's stepmother, a role proverbial for meanness.

3.43–44   Pliny the Elder (*Historia naturalis* 36.6) tells how Marcus Aemilius Scaurus ordered the choicest of the marble columns from his temporary theater stage dragged through the Forum up to his residence on the Palatine Hill.

3.45–46   By the time of Augustus, wealthy Romans began cutting off part of their villas' sea frontage with breakwaters to form fish ponds.

3.59–60   This is to say that he had once been a slave whose feet would have been coated with chalk when he was displayed for sale.

3.78   The sign of a dandy. Cf. Tibullus 1.6.18.

4.16–18   That is, to sing epic or didactic poetry.

4.49–50   A poetic variant of the prayer "Sit terra tibi levis," abbreviated STTL, regularly found on Roman sepulchral monuments.

4.57–58   See above on Tibullus 2.1.68.

5   The poem is a long celebration of the induction of Messallinus, eldest son of Tibullus's patron, Messalla, into the Quindecimviri Sacris Faciundis, a college of priests whose duty it was to guard the Sibylline Books and consult them when asked by the Senate. The date is most likely ca. 20 B.C.E.

5.1–4 and following   Tibullus may be thinking of the statue of Apollo Citharoedus that graced the Temple of Apollo dedicated by Augustus on the Palatine in 28 B.C.E.

5.9–10   Tibullus is referring to the defeat of the Titans, one of whose principal members was Cronus (Saturn), by Zeus (Jupiter, Jove). A contemporary Roman would have called to mind the defeat of Antony and Cleopatra at Actium in 31 B.C.E. by Octavian, soon to adopt the name Augustus.

5.16   The Sibylline Oracles were written in (Greek) hexameters.

5.19–20　According to Tibullus a Sibyl prophesied to Aeneas soon after the fall of Troy, not after his arrival in Italy (as Virgil would have it in *Aeneid* 6), that Rome was in his future.

5.26　The Capitolium (the modern Capitoline), from the eastern crest of which the grand temple to Jupiter Optimus Maximus faced out over the Forum Romanum.

5.48　The death of Turnus is the subject of the final scene of Virgil's *Aeneid*. The epithet that Tibullus has the Sibyl give him (*barbarus*) could be variously interpreted as signifying foreign, uncouth, or savage.

5.71–78　A description of the portents that appeared after the murder of Julius Caesar on the Ides of March 44 B.C.E. (See also a parallel list in Virgil *Georgics* 1.466–88.)

5.115–16　Floats representing conquered towns were carried in the triumphal procession.

6.25–26　Tibullus refers to the chain gangs of slaves who worked the land.

6.40　Virgil is fond of using the word *lacus* to describe the various waters of the Underworld.

LYGDAMUS

1.1 and following　The feast of the Matronalia, at which presents were offered to married women and brides, was celebrated on March 1. Mars, as father of Romulus and Remus, was considered the founding god of Rome.

1.9–14　A detailed look at how a selection of Roman poetry would have been presented as a papyrus roll. Compare Catullus 22.5–8.

3.15　See also Horace *Carmina* 3.10.5–6 and *Epistles* 1.10.22 for extravagant gardens built within a Roman house's peristyle.

3.34　The most famous pictorial example of Venus on her shell is Sandro Botticelli's *Birth of Venus* (1485). For an ancient depiction of the scene, see the wall painting in the Casa della Venere in Conchiglia, Pompeii.

4.5–6　Etruscan priests were notorious for their powers of divination.

4.10　There is a creative interaction here with Horace *Carmina* 1.23.10 ("farre pio placant et saliente mica"). Lygdamus opts for the final alliteration, which the lyric poet avoids.

4.23–38　Portrait of Apollo.

4.31–34　The lines are reminiscent of the similes Virgil uses to describe Lavinia's blush at *Aeneid* 12.67–69.

4.71　Though the text is difficult, the line clearly imitates Virgil *Eclogue* 1.2. While Apollo was serving as herdsman for Admetus, the poetry that he sang was appropriately pastoral. Cf. also the setting and language of Tibullus 2.1.53.

4.87–88　Cerberus is meant, the dog guarding the entrance to the Underworld.

5.1–2　Among possible locations are modern Cerveteri, Bracciano, and Bolsena.

5.7–8　The rites of the Bona Dea are meant. See also Tibullus 2.6.22.

5.18   Reference is to the battle of Mutina in 43 B.C.E., where both consuls, Hirtius and Pansa, fell. The relation of this line to *Tristia* 4.10.6, where Ovid tells of his own birth in parallel language, has been much debated.

5.22   When Jupiter, Neptune, and Pluto cast lots for the rule of heaven, earth, and Underworld, Pluto gained control of the last of the trio.

5.29–30   Lygdamus may be referring to the famous springs and fountain of Clitumnus, near modern Assisi. See commentators on Propertius 2.19.25–26.

6.8   Probably a reference to birds of good omen. Compare the use of "snow-bright" at Lygdamus 3.25 above.

6.41   Gaius Valerius Catullus (ca. 84 B.C.E.–ca. 54 B.C.E.) was one of Rome's greatest lyric poets. Ariadne's desertion is a major subject of his longest poem (*Carmen* 64), written in hexameters.

Glossary

ADMETUS   King of Pherae, husband of Alcestis and lover of Apollo.

AEGEAN   Sea between mainland Greece and Asia Minor.

AENEAS   Son of Venus and Anchises; hero of Virgil's *Aeneid,* who journeyed from Troy to Italy and is considered the ancestral founder of Rome.

AFRICA   Northern segment of the modern continent, part of which constituted a Roman province.

ALBA *or* ALBA LONGA   Ancient city of Latium in the hills east of Rome.

AMALTHEA   Apparently the Sibyl who sold the Sibylline Books to King Tarquinius Priscus.

AMOR   Roman personification of love.

ANIAN   Connected with the Anio (the modern Aniene), a river of Latium entering the Tiber north of Rome.

APOLLO   Greek and Roman god of the bow and the lyre, leader of the Muses and patron of poets; also called Phoebus, from his role as god of the sun, or Delian, from his place of birth, the island of Delos.

AQUITANIA *and* AQUITANI   Country and its people located in southwestern Gaul.

ARABIA *and* ARABES   Arabia and its people, known in antiquity for incense.

ARAR   The modern river Saône.

ARMENIA   Asian country north of ancient Mesopotamia.

ARRETIUM   Etrurian town in the upper Tiber valley, the modern Arezzo.

ASCANIUS   Son of Aeneas, founder of Alba Longa; also called Iulus.

ASSYRIA   Region in Mesopotamia located in the northern Tigris Valley, now largely modern Iraq.

ATAX   The modern river Aude.

AURORA   Roman personification of the dawn of day (the Greek Eos).

AUSTER   The Southwest Wind.

AVERNUS   Lake northwest of Naples, supposedly an entranceway into the Underworld and often standing for it.

BACCHUS   Roman vegetation god (the Greek Dionysus) whose special province was the vine; often treated metonymically as wine itself. He is called Lenaeus as god of the wine press and Liber and Lyaeus in his role as the one who "frees" through wine.

BAIAE   Modern Baia, a seaside resort area northwest of Naples beloved in antiquity by Roman gentry. See *Elegy* 1.11 of Tibullus's contemporary elegist Propertius.

BELLONA   Roman personification of war.

BONA DEA   The "Good Goddess," a Roman deity of Italian origin worshipped exclusively by women.

CADMEAN   Theban, in reference to Cadmus, the founder of Thebes. His daughter Agave was the mother of Pentheus, a Theban king torn apart by Bacchants for scorning their god.

CALVUS (GAIUS LICINIUS CALVUS, 82–CA. 47 B.C.E.)   Orator and neoteric poet of the late Roman Republic, friend of Catullus.

CAMENAE   Roman water deities who became equivalent to the Greek Muses and often stand for poetry itself.

CAMPANIA   Italian province south of Latium noted for its fertility.

CANIS   *See* Sirius.

CARNUTI   Gallic tribe dwelling near the Liger (the modern Loire).

CARYSTUS   Town on the southern coast of the Aegean island of Euboea, famed as a source for cipollino marble.

CASTALIA   Spring below Mount Parnassus sacred to Apollo and the Muses.

CATULLUS   *See note to Lygdamus 6.41.*

CERBERUS   Monstrous three-headed dog, guardian of the entrance to Hades.

CERES   Roman goddess of grain, associated with the Greek Demeter and often standing for the land itself and its produce.

CERINTHUS   Lover of Sulpicia, who disguises his real name with a Greek pseudonym in her poetry.

CHIMAERA   Mythical monster, part lion, part dragon, part goat.

CHIOS; CHIAN   Aegean island famous for its wine; associated with that island.

CILICES   Inhabitants of the Roman province of Cilicia, in southeastern Asia Minor, site of an expedition by Messalla after the battle of Actium in 31 B.C.E.

CIMMERIAN   Epithet of the Underworld, derived from the name of a semi-mythical people living beyond the Black Sea.

CIRCE   Sea nymph famous from Homer on for her magic powers.

CNOSSOS   Cretan birthplace of Ariadne, daughter of King Minos.

CORNUTUS   Friend of Tibullus and probable associate of his patron, Messalla Corvinus.

COS; COAN   Aegean island that produced a transparent type of cloth; associated with that island.

CRONUS   *See* Saturn.

CUMAE; CUMAEAN   Coastal town in Campania north of Naples; associated with that town. It was the seat of the famous Cumaean Sibyl and was known for unpretentious tableware, usually called Campanian.

CUPID (LATIN *CUPIDO*)   Son of Venus, the Roman personification of carnal desire.

CYDNUS   The modern Berdan, a river in Cilicia, in what is now southwestern Turkey.

CYNTHUS   The mountain of the island of Delos.

CYPRIA   *See* Venus.

CYTHERA *or* CYTHEREA   *See* Venus.

DANAIDS   Daughters of Danaus, who murdered their cousin-husbands on their wedding night and suffer eternal torture in the Underworld.

DELIA   Name of Tibullus's mistress, derived from one of the epithets of Diana.

DELOS; DELIAN   Aegean island, birthplace of Apollo and Diana; associated with that island.

DELPHIC   Associated with Delphi, a town in Phocis, the site of one of Apollo's chief shrines.

DIANA   Roman goddess of the moon and of hunting, the Greek Artemis. As Trivia, worshipped at crossroads (*trivium*), she is associated with magic, the occult, and the Underworld.

DICTYNNA ("LADY OF THE NET")   Cretan nymph whose cult was assimilated to that of Artemis-Diana.

DIS   In Roman religion, the ruler of the Underworld.

DOMITIUS MARSUS   A writer, primarily of epigrams, of the time of Augustus. His couplets on the contemporaneous deaths of Virgil and Tibullus in the year 19 B.C.E. form part of a digest of Suetonius's *vita* of the elegist.

ELIS   Area in the northwestern Peloponnesus where the Olympic Games were held.

ELYSIUM; ELYSIAN   The Greek and Roman abode of the blessed after death; associated with that place. An Elysium for lovers with Venus as its guide may be Tibullus's invention.

EOS; EOAN   The East; Eastern. From the Greek word for "dawn."

ERYTHRAEA   Connected with the *mare Erythrum,* the modern Arabian Sea.

ERYX   Mountain in northwestern Sicily famous for its temple to Venus.

ETRUSCAN   From the Italian region of Etruria, west of the Apennines, the precursor of modern Tuscany.

EURUS   The East Wind.

FALERNUS; FALERNIAN   The *ager Falernus,* between Rome and Naples, which produced some of ancient Italy's finest wines; associated with that locality.

FORS   The Roman personification of chance, allied to Fortuna.

FORTUNA   The Roman personification of fortune, who had several temples in Rome but whose most famous shrine was at Praeneste (modern Palestrina), in the hills to the east of the city.

GALLUS (GAIUS CORNELIUS GALLUS, 70/69–27/6 B.C.E.)   Poet, statesman, friend of Augustus; usually placed chronologically first in the list of Roman writers of elegiac verse.

GARUNNA   The modern river Garonne.

GENIUS   In Roman belief, the inner spirit of an individual or a family.

GRAIAN   Associated with Greece, the land of the Greeks.

HAEMONIA   An old name for Thessaly, whose southern segment was ruled over by Peleus, the father of Achilles.

HECATE   The Underworld aspect of a triform goddess (Luna in heaven, Artemis-Diana on Earth). She is also called Trivia for her association with crossroads (*trivium*) and is regularly accompanied by dogs.

HEROPHILE   Supposedly the name of the Erythraean Sibyl, who came from Marpessus, near Troy.

IDA   Phrygian mountain range near Troy, associated with the worship of Cybele, the Great Mother.

ILIA   Roman priestess of Vesta raped by Mars. She became the mother of Romulus and Remus.

ILION   The Greek form for Latin *Ilium,* another name for Troy.

INDIA; INDI   Land vaguely coterminous with the modern subcontinent; its inhabitants.

INDIGES   Title given Aeneas after his death, probably meaning "Native God."

ISIS Egyptian fertility goddess whose cult was popular among Roman women from the early first century B.C.E. on.

ISMARA Mountain range in southern Thrace.

IULUS *See* Ascanius.

IXION Like Tityos, Tantalus, and the Danaids, a mortal regularly listed among the damned in the Underworld, in this case punished for trying to seduce Hera-Juno.

JUNO Roman goddess (the Greek Hera), daughter of Saturn and wife of Jupiter. From her role as *pronuba,* who conducted the bride to the marriage chamber, she was the goddess of weddings.

JUPITER (JOVE) The Greek Zeus, chief god of the Olympian pantheon, in his role as Jupiter Pluvius, the dispenser of rain.

KALENDS First day of any Roman month.

LARES (SG. LAR) Roman tutelary divinities, usually guardians of hearth and home.

LATONA Roman name of the Greek Leto, mother of Apollo and of Diana.

LAURENTIA Belonging to Laurentum, a coastal town south of Ostia in Latium, where Aeneas landed.

LAVINIUM City in Latium founded by Aeneas and named after his wife Lavinia.

LENAEUS *See* Bacchus.

LETHAEAN Of Lethe, a fountain in the Underworld. To drink its waters brought forgetfulness.

LIBER *See* Bacchus.

LIGER The modern river Loire.

LINUS Mythical poet, son of Apollo.

LUCIFER ("BRINGER OF LIGHT") Venus as the Morning Star.

LUCINA Roman personification, bringer of light and life, often identified with Diana or Juno.

LUNA *See* Diana.

LYAEUS *See* Bacchus.

LYDIA Country in western Asia Minor whose main river, the Pactolus, was supposedly gold-bearing.

MACER The identity of the poet's friend is uncertain. He is possibly the addressee of Ovid *Amores* 2.6 and *Epistulae ex Ponto* 2.10.

MAEONIA Area in eastern Lydia, supposedly the birthplace of Homer.

MANES Roman spirits of the dead, considered to have quasi-divine powers.

MARATHUS   *Puer delicatus* who appears in Tibullus's *Elegies* 1.4, 1.8, and, by implication, 1.9.

MARCIA, MARCIAN   *Aqua Marcia* was water brought into Rome on the aqueduct built by Quintus Marcius Rex in 144–140 B.C.E.

MARS   The Roman god of war, often standing for war itself.

MEDEA   Tragic heroine, lover of Jason, renowned as a sorceress.

MEMNON   Son of Aurora and Tithonus who dies at Troy.

MEMPHIS   City in Lower Egypt, site of a famous temple to Osiris whose incarnation was Apis, the Bull God.

MESSALLINUS   Marcus Valerius Messalla Messallinus (consul 3 B.C.E.), eldest son of Messalla Corvinus.

MESSALLA   *See note to Tibullus 1.3.1.*

MINERVA   A Roman equivalent of the Greek Athena, goddess of handicrafts and, more generally, of wisdom.

MINOS   *See* Ariadne.

MOPSOPIA; MOPSOPIAN   Another name for Attica, known for its honey from Mount Hymettus; associated with that locality.

MORS   Roman personification of death.

MUSES   Goddesses who preside over the arts, especially poetry; also called Pierides, from Pieria, an area in Greece north of Mount Olympus.

NAIAD   Water nymph, often standing for water itself.

NATALIS   Roman birthday spirit, closely parallel to one's Genius.

NEAERA   Mistress of Lygdamus.

NEMESIS   From the Greek personification of revenge, the name that Tibullus gives to the girl who is the subject of several elegies of his second book.

NEREID   Sea nymph, daughter of the sea god Nereus.

NILUS   The modern Nile, the central river of Egypt.

NISUS   King of Megara and father of Scylla, who cut off a lock of his hair upon which his life depended.

NOTUS (PL. NOTI)   The South Wind.

NOX   Roman personification of night.

NUMICUS *and* NUMICIUS   A river of Latium (the modern rio Torto) next to which Aeneas was supposedly buried; also (Numicius) associated with that river.

OCEAN (LATIN *OCEANUS*)   The Greek Okeanos: for the ancients the water, especially the modern Atlantic, surrounding the known landmass.

OLYMPUS   Mountain in northern Greece considered the home of the gods.

OPS   Roman personification of plenty, the wife of Saturn. She was linked with Rhea, whose cult in turn was associated with the Phrygian goddess Cybele.

ORCUS   Another name for Dis, the Roman god of the Underworld.

OSIRIS   Egyptian god identified with the Nile, the husband and brother of Isis.

PALATIUM   The modern Palatine, one of Rome's central hills and the site of its initial settlement, which gave its name to the imperial residences ("palaces") situated on it.

PALES   Roman tutelary deity of flocks and herds.

PALAESTINE   Largely, modern Palestine, country of the Jews in biblical times, located within Syria.

PAN   An Arcadian god of shepherds and woods, often identified with the Roman Silvanus.

PANCHAIA   A mythical island in the Indian Ocean renowned for its incense.

PARCAE   The Roman Fates, equivalent to the Greek Moirai, who foretold human destiny.

PARILIA (PALILIA)   Festival in honor of Pales held on April 21, the traditional date of the foundation of Rome.

PAX   Roman personification of peace.

PELEUS   Son of Aeacus, husband of Thetis and father of Achilles.

PELOPS   King of Phrygia whose ivory shoulder replaced one mistakenly eaten by Demeter when he was dismembered by his father, Tantalus.

PENATES   Roman tutelary divinities, especially the guardians of house and larder.

PERSEPHONE   Greek name for the Roman Proserpina, wife of Pluto, god of the Underworld.

PHAEACIA   Island off the northwestern coast of Greece, home of Homer's Phaeacians (it is called Scherie in the *Odyssey*); also thought to be Corcyra, the modern Corfù.

PHARIAN   From Pharos, an island at the entrance to the harbor of Alexandria famous for its lighthouse; also a center for the cult of Isis. It stands often by metonymy for Egypt itself.

PHOEBUS   *See* Apollo.

PHOETO   The Sibyl from the island of Samos.

PHOLOE   The name of a girl in an ode of Horace (*Carmina* 1.33) probably also addressed to Tibullus.

PHRYGIA   Country in western Asia Minor by metonymy often associated with Troy. It was known for its white marble with purple markings and for a musical mode that bears its name.

PHRYNE   Name of a procuress. ("Toad" in Greek.)

PIERIA, PIERIDES   *See* Muses.

POENA   Roman equivalent of Poine, the Greek personification of punishment and revenge.

PRIAPUS   Son of Dionysus and Aphrodite, a fertility god noted for his prominent phallus. His particular province was the protection of gardens.

PYRENE   The Pyrenees, the mountain chain serving as the border between modern France and Spain.

PYTHO   An old name for Delphi.

REMUS   Twin brother of Romulus, killed by him at the time of Rome's founding.

RHODANUS   The modern river Rhône.

ROME   City on the Tiber, metropolis of the Roman Empire.

ROMULUS   Founder of the city of Rome.

RUTULI; RUTULIAN   Ancient tribe of Latium whose capital was Ardea; associated with that people.

SAMOS; SAMIAN   An Aegean island that produced inexpensive tableware; associated with that island.

SANTONI   A Gallic tribe dwelling near the mouth of the Garunna.

SATURN   An ancient Roman god of agriculture, usually identified with the Greek Kronos (Latin *Cronus*). His reign was often considered the Golden Age.

SATURNIA   *See* Juno.

SCYLLA   Sea monster whose lair was the modern Straits of Messina.

SCYTHIA   Land of a nomadic tribe north of the Black Sea.

SEMELE   Mother of Bacchus/Dionysus, whose father was Zeus/Jupiter.

SERVIUS   Servius Sulpicius Rufus (ca. 106–43 B.C.E.), father of Sulpicia.

SIBYL   Name given to several female prophets; in Tibullus referring probably to the one located at Cumae who served as Aeneas's guide through the Underworld in Book 6 of the *Aeneid*.

SIDON   Town on the coast of Phoenicia known for its dyeing industry.

SILVANUS   A Roman god associated equally with woods and farmland.

SIRIUS   The Dog Star, most prominent feature in the constellation Canis Major (the Great Dog), one of the brightest in the night sky. Its rising often marked the commencement of summer heat.

SOL   For the Romans, the sun, often personified.

SOMNUS   Roman personification of sleep, the Greek Hypnos. Perhaps his most dramatic appearance in Latin poetry is at Virgil *Aeneid* 5.838–61. Dreams (Somnia) are his companions.

SPES (HOPE)   Abstraction worshipped as a goddess whose chief Roman temple was in the Forum Holitorium.

STYX; STYGIAN   Principal river of the Underworld; associated with that river.

SYRIA; SYRIAN   Country between Egypt and Asia Minor, exporter of myrrh; associated with that country.

SYRTIS   Treacherous shallow waters off the coast of Libya.

TAENARUS   Cape at the extreme southwestern peninsula of the Peloponessus, known as a source of rosso antico marble.

TANTALUS   Traditional wrongdoer, according to the fifth-century C.E. historian Orosius (1.12.4) punished in the Underworld for raping Ganymede.

TARBELLI   A people dwelling in the southern part of Aquitania.

TAURUS   Mountain range in southern Asia minor, the modern Bulgar Dagh.

THESEUS   Athenian hero who abandoned Ariadne on the Aegean island of Naxos. *See also* Cnossos.

THESSALY (THESSALIA)   Region of northern Greece south of Macedonia, land of magic par excellence.

THETIS   Sea nymph, the wife of Peleus and mother of Achilles.

TIBURS   The Sibyl from Tibur (modern Tivoli), a city east of Rome on the Anio River.

TISIPHONE ("AVENGER OF MURDER")   For the Greeks, one of the three Furies, personified spirits of revenge.

TITIUS   Perhaps the poet whom Horace mentions at *Epistles* 1.3.9–11 as emulating Pindar.

TITYOS   A Giant regularly singled out, like Ixion and Tantalus, as an offender against the gods, punished in the Underworld for attempting to violate Latona.

TRIVIA   *See* Diana *and* Hecate.

TROY; TROJAN   City in northwestern Asia Minor, scene of Homer's *Iliad,* whence Aeneas departed for Rome; associated with that city.

TURNUS   Chief of the Rutuli and prime opponent of Aeneas.

TUSCAN   Associated with Etruria (modern Tuscany).

TUSCULUM   A town of Latium in the Alban Hills east of Rome.

TYROS   Modern Tyre, an important trading city on the coast of Phoenicia known for its production of purple dye.

VALGIUS   If C. G. Heyne's emendation of the manuscripts' reading *vulgi* is correct, probably Gaius Valgius Rufus, consul of 12 B.C.E., friend of Horace and writer of elegy and epic.

VELABRUM   A district of ancient Rome between the Forum Romanum and the Tiber River.

VENUS (CYPRIA)   The Roman goddess of love (equivalent to the Greek Aphrodite), born from the foam created when Kronos (Latin *Cronus*) castrated his father, Uranus (the Greek Ouranos), and threw the genitals into the Aegean Sea near the island of Cythera (Kythera), toward which she floated on a shell. Cyprus, equally renowned for her worship, was also named as her destination.

VESTA   The Roman goddess of the domestic hearth, the Greek Hestia.

VICTORIA   The Roman personification of victory, the Greek Nike.

VULCAN   The Roman god of fire, the Greek Hephaistos.

Select Bibliography

Titles of journals are abbreviated as in the frontmatter of S. Hornblower and A. Spawforth, eds., *The Oxford Classical Dictionary,* 3rd edition, revised (Oxford, 2003), and the annual issues of *L'Année Philologique.*

Ball, R., *Tibullus the Elegist: A Critical Survey.* Göttingen, 1983.

Boyd, B. W. "*Parva seges satis est:* The Landscape of Tibullan Elegy in 1.1 and 1.10." *TAPhA* 114 (1984): 273–80.

Bright, D. " A Tibullan Odyssey." *Arethusa* 4 (1971): 197–214.

———."The Art and Structure of Tibullus 1.7." *Grazer Beiträge* 3 (1975): 31–46.

———. Haec mihi fingebam: *Tibullus in His World.* Leiden, 1978.

Bulloch, A. W. "Tibullus and the Alexandrians." *PCPhS* 19 (1973): 71–89.

Butrica, J. L. "Messalla and the Principate." In Carl Deroux, ed., *Studies in Latin Literature and Roman History,* vol. 7, 279–96. Brussels, 1994.

Cairns, F. "Ancient 'Etymology' and Tibullus: On the Classification of 'Etymologies' and on 'Etymological Markers.'" *PCPhS* 42 (1996): 24–59.

———. "Tibullus 2.2." *Papers of the Leeds International Latin Seminar* 10 (1998): 203–34.

———. *Tibullus: A Hellenistic Poet at Rome.* Cambridge, 1979.

Carrier, C., trans. *The Poems of Tibullus.* Bloomington, 1968.

Dawson, C. "An Alexandrian Prototype of Marathus?" *AJPh* 67 (1946): 1–15.

Elder, J. P. "Tibullus: *Tersus atque elegans.*" In J. P. Sullivan, ed., *Critical Essays on Roman Literature* 65–105. Cambridge, 1962.

Flaschenriem, B. "Sulpicia and the Rhetoric of Disclosure." *CPh* 94 (1999): 36–54.

Gaisser, J. "Structure and Tone in Tibullus 1.6." *AJPh* 92 (1971): 202–16.

———. "Tibullus 1.7: A Tribute to Messalla." *CPh* 66 (1971): 221–29.

———. "Tibullus 2.3 and Vergil's Tenth *Eclogue.*" *TAPhA* 107 (1977): 131–46.

———. "*Amor, rura* and *militia* in Three Elegies of Tibullus (1.1, 1.5 and 1.10)." *Latomus* 42 (1983): 58–72.

Harrauer, H. *A Bibliography to the Corpus Tibullianum.* Hildesheim, 1971.

Hinds, S. "The Poetess and the Reader: Further Steps towards Sulpicia." *Hermathena* 143 (1987): 29–46.

Hollis, A. *Fragments of Roman Poetry c. 60 B.C.–A.D. 20.* Oxford, 2007.

Holzberg, N. *Die römische Liebeselegie: Eine Einführung.* Darmstadt, 1990.

Hutchinson, G. O. *Hellenistic Poetry.* Oxford, 1988.

James, S. *Learned Girls and Male Persuasion: Gender and Reading in Roman Love Elegy.* Berkeley and Los Angeles, 2003.

Johnson, W. R. "Messalla's Birthday: The Politics of Pastoral." *Arethusa* 23 (1990): 95–113.

Katz, V. "Translating Roman Elegy." In B. Gold, ed., *Blackwell Companion to Roman Love Elegy* 234–50. Oxford, 2011.

Knox, P. E. "Milestones in the Career of Tibullus." *CQ* 55 (2005): 204–16.

Lattimore, R. *Themes in Greek and Latin Epitaphs.* Urbana, 1962.

Leach, E. W. "Vergil, Horace, Tibullus: Three Collections of Ten," *Ramus* 7 (1978): 79–105.

———. "Poetics and Poetic Design in Tibullus' First Elegiac Book." *Arethusa* 13 (1980): 79–96.

———. "Sacral-Idyllic Landscape Painting and the Poems of Tibullus' First Book." *Latomus* 39 (1980): 47–69.

———. "Rome's Elegiac Cartography: The View from the *Via Sacra,* Center and Periphery." In B. Gold, ed., *Blackwell Companion to Roman Love Elegy* 134–51. Oxford, 2011.

Lee, G., ed. and trans. *Tibullus: Elegies.* Cambridge, 1975. [3rd edition (with R. Maltby): Leeds, 1990.]

Lee-Stecum, P. *Powerplay in Tibullus: Reading Elegies Book One.* Cambridge, 1998.

Lenz, F. W., and G. K. Galinsky, eds. *Albii Tibulli aliorumque carminum libri tres.* Leiden, 1971.

Lowe, N. "Sulpicia's Syntax." *CQ* 38 (1988): 193–205.

Luck, G. *The Latin Love Elegy.* 2nd ed. London, 1969.

———, ed. *Albii Tibulli aliorumque carmina.* Stuttgart, 1988.

Lyne, R. O. A. M. *The Latin Love Poets from Catullus to Horace.* Oxford, 1980.

———. "Propertius and Tibullus: Early Exchanges." *CQ* 48 (1998): 519–44. [Reprinted in *Collected Papers on Latin Poetry,* ed. G. O. Hutchinson and S. Harrison (Oxford, 2007), 251–82.]

———. "*Servitium amoris.*" *CQ* 29 (1979): 117–30.

Maltby, R. *Tibullus: Elegies.* Cambridge, 2002.

Miller, P. A., ed. *Latin Erotic Elegy.* London, 2002.

———. *Subjecting Verses: Latin Love Elegy and the Emergence of the Real.* Princeton, 2004.

———. "Tibullus." In B. Gold, ed., *Blackwell Companion to Roman Love Elegy.* 53–69. Oxford, 2011.

———. *Tibullus.* Wauconda, 2012.

Murgatroyd, P. "*Militia amoris* and the Roman Elegists." *Latomus* 34 (1975): 59–79.

———, ed. *Tibullus I: A Commentary.* Pietermaritzburg, 1980. [Reprint: Bristol, 1991.]

———. *Tibullus: Elegies II.* Oxford, 1994.

Mutschler, F.-H. *Die poetische Kunst Tibulls*. Frankfurt, 1985.

Navarro Antolín, F., ed. *Lygdamus, Corpus Tibullianum III.1–6: Lygdami elegiarum liber*. Leiden, 1996.

O'Hara, J. *True Names: Vergil and the Alexandrian Tradition of Etymological Wordplay*. Ann Arbor, 1996.

Postgate, J. P. *Selections from Tibullus and Others*. London, 1903. [3rd ed.: London, 1929.]

Putnam, M. C. J. "Simple Tibullus and the Ruse of Style." *Yale French Studies* 45 (1970): 21–32: [Reprinted in *Essays on Latin Lyric, Elegy and Epic* (Princeton, 1982), 163–74.]

———. "Horace and Tibullus." *CPh* 67 (1972): 81–88. [Reprinted in *Essays on Latin Lyric, Elegy and Epic* (Princeton, 1982), 152–59.]

———. *Tibullus: A Commentary*. Norman, 1973.

———. "Virgil and Tibullus 1.1." *CPh* 100 (2005): 123–41.

Ramsby, T. R. *Textual Permanence: Roman Elegists and the Epigraphic Tradition*. London, 2007.

Santirocco, M. "Sulpicia Reconsidered." *CJ* 74 (1979): 229–39.

Smith, K. F. *The Elegies of Albius Tibullus*. New York, 1913. [Reprint: Darmstadt, 1964.]

Syme, R. *The Augustan Aristocracy*. Oxford, 1986.

———. "A Great Orator Mislaid." *CQ* 31 (1981): 421–27. [Reprinted in A. Birley, ed., *Roman Papers*, vol. 3 (Oxford, 1984), 1417–22.]

Taylor, L. R. "Republican and Augustan Writers Enrolled in the Equestrian Centuries." *TAPhA* 99 (1968): 469–86.

Tränkle, H. *Appendix Tibulliana*. (Berlin, 1990).

Veyne, P. *Roman Erotic Elegy: Love, Poetry, and the West*. Chicago, 1988. [Translation by D. Pellauer of *L'élégie érotique romaine: L'amour, la poésie et l'occident* (Paris, 1983).]

White, P. *Promised Verse: Poets in the Society of Augustan Rome*. Cambridge, 1993.

Wimmel, W. *Der frühe Tibull*. Munich, 1968.

Zanker, P. *The Power of Images in the Age of Augustus*. Ann Arbor, 1988. [Translation by A. Shapiro of *Augustus und die Macht der Bilder* (Munich, 1987).]

Index

In this index, the abbreviations "v" and "vv" represent the words "verse" and "verses," respectively; likewise, "n" and "nn" represent "note" and "notes." An "f" after a page number indicates a separate reference, or separate references, on the next page; an "ff" indicates separate references on the next two pages. "Passim" indicates a cluster of references in close but not necessarily consecutive page sequence.

Text 10.25/13 Garamond Premium Pro   *Display* Garamond Premium Pro
Compositor BookMatters, Berkeley   *Indexer* Paul Psoinos
Printer and binder Maple-Vail Book Manufacturing Group
∎